EMBEDDED

on the **Home Front**

EMBEDDED

on the Home Front

WHERE MILITARY AND CIVILIAN LIVES CONVERGE

EDITED BY

JOAN DIXON AND BARB HOWARD

VICTORIA | VANCOUVER | CALGARY

Heritage House Publishing Company Ltd.
heritagehouse.ca

LIBRARY AND ARCHIVES CANADA CATALOGUING IN PUBLICATION
Embedded on the home front: where military and civilian lives converge / edited by Joan Dixon and Barb Howard.

Issued also in electronic format.
ISBN 978-1-927051-57-3

    1. Canadian prose literature (English)—21st century. 2. War in literature. 3. War and society. 4. Peace-building, Canadian, in literature. 5. Veterans in literature. 6. Soldiers in literature. I. Dixon, Joan, 1957– II. Howard, Barb, 1962–

PS8367.W3E43 2012   C814.60803581   C2012-903833-4

Copy edited by Christine Savage
Proofread by Lara Kordic
Cover and book design by Jacqui Thomas
Cover photo: Corporal Auger is greeted by his children at Jean-Lesage International Airport in
    Quebec City, March 22, 2010. Photographed by Corporal Roxanne Shewchuk
Cover and interior wallpaper: Electric_Crayon/iStockphoto.com

 The interior of this book was produced on 100% post-consumer recycled paper, processed chlorine free and printed with vegetable-based inks.

Heritage House acknowledges the financial support for its publishing program from the Government of Canada through the Canada Book Fund (CBF), Canada Council for the Arts and the province of British Columbia through the British Columbia Arts Council and the Book Publishing Tax Credit.

 Canadian Heritage   Patrimoine canadien

 The Canada Council | Le Conseil des Arts
for the Arts | du Canada

 BRITISH COLUMBIA ARTS COUNCIL

16 15 14 13 12 1 2 3 4 5
Printed in Canada

Canadians, if they are not serving in the Forces, if they are not family members of those who do or if they do not live near a military base, seem to have been able to put the war in a box.

ALISON HOWELL
author of *Madness in International Relations*

We have a duty to be honest and rigorous, with ourselves and with others, and to be able to brook contradiction and argument in our discussions of past wars and the present one in Afghanistan.

NOAH RICHLER
What We Talk About When We Talk About War

CONTENTS

INTRODUCTION

The military home front.

A few years ago, neither of us knew much about this subset of our community—even though we were both accidental members. One of us was the didn't-see-it-coming mother of a deploying soldier; the other was the clueless daughter of a peacetime reservist general. As colleagues in the writing biz, we naturally sought out literature for insight. When we couldn't find a book or anthology on the topic, we decided to build one.

Defining the military home front was trickier than we expected. The home front in the First and Second World Wars was an integral part of the nation's war effort; everyone who wasn't on the war front overseas was on the home front. Easy. But more recently, during times of peacekeeping, peacemaking or armed interventions and conflict, the notion of home front seems to comprise only those who are in some way directly associated with or related to the military: family and friends of soldiers, returning soldiers, ex-soldiers. Today's home front is a minority group, often invisible or camouflaged by everyday jobs and activities. It is to these people that we looked to build a collage of personal narratives that would explore the home front and help to enlighten us.

The writers in this book (essayists, novelists, journalists, poets) have found themselves at one time or another, voluntarily or not, embedded on the military home front as witnesses. After benefitting from their courageous and intelligent narratives, we now define the military home front as an area of nexus—where military life interconnects, sometimes collides, with civilian life. Often these areas of convergence are the crux of the essays. Battles and collateral damage, for instance, are common to both fronts, as are notions of "brotherhood," duty and pride.

Each home front experience is unique, and each home front story in this collection comes from a single perspective with its own theme. However, several motifs surfaced. A concept of family, for instance, is found in every essay, be that family in the nature of blood, military unit, colleague or romantic partner. Along with literal images (snapshots, studio portraits and the televised horrors of 9/11) are the recurring concepts of fate and death—and the mental and physical fallout these bring to the home front. Several of the stories deal with survivors adapting to new or different worlds: military and civilian, before and after a death.

To represent every avenue and aspect of the military home front would be an impossible task. We have only chipped into the vast supply of worthy stories, but this collection captures triumphs and incredible fortitude, humour and grief, as well as the illogic, the fears, the anger and other everyday realities of home front life. It includes the voices of many generations and frontline reflections on:

- growing up military, and joining or rejecting the family "business"

- losing a child or being widowed due to military involvement, or worrying about these possibilities every day

- observing how the Canadian and American military home fronts differ

- returning to the home front after serving on the war front

- remembering and remembrance, and what these terms mean to the people who are connected to those who serve in the Canadian Forces.

Finally, several years after our first home front conversation, we invite you to grab your beverage of choice and settle in for a unique read. Why a beverage? Because drinking figures prominently on the military home front, and booze or coffee spills into or out of most of the stories, whether in the context of socializing, celebrating, memorializing or remembrance.

Still embedded on the home front,
Joan Dixon and Barb Howard

YELLOW RIBBONS

Nancy McAllister

Tie a yellow ribbon. I remember the phrase well from a song on the truly terrible radio station my mother used to listen to when I was young. I never had any idea what it meant. Several decades later, with children of my own questioning my taste in music, I have a brother stationed with the NATO forces in Kandahar Province, Afghanistan, and I know all about those yellow ribbons and what they have come to represent to families awaiting the return of soldiers abroad.

My big brother, Dave, returns home from his latest tour in Afghanistan in just a few days; nine months have passed since he left on that mission. I am keen to see him home and safe, but I am surprised to realize that I've gotten used to him being gone. You can get used to anything, no matter how far from normal it might be.

It isn't the first time we've had to wait at home for him. Dave spent much of 2006 at Kandahar Airfield. This time around, he was in an apparently less dangerous but more secretive location: he was running a small base in the middle of nowhere, in a country with a great deal of nowhere. During his previous tour, there were quite a few tired, slightly dejected phone calls home, often after one of the many casualty reports that frequented the daily news.

This time, Dave's calls were more upbeat, and we saw many emailed photos of him and his smiling colleagues and their equally cheerful counterparts in the Afghan army. I knew they were still under pressure to get local recruits trained and ready for the national police force. But the violence in Kandahar Province had been convincingly subdued, and much of their focus could turn toward nation-building rather than constant fighting.

Dave always looked pretty out of place when he stood next to the Afghan locals. At six foot three he's taller than many Canadians, but he seems to tower over all Afghans. He seemed even more incongruous in a photo taken during a local function, in which he is sporting the traditional outfit of *shalwar kameez*—a long tunic over slightly cropped trousers—looking like a giant in short pyjamas.

My parents and I have been fortunate in that Dave tends to spend his time inside the wire; he does not go on foot patrol or ride around in armoured convoys as must many of his colleagues. I suspect that their unlucky families have felt their stomachs lurch each time they heard of an as-yet-unnamed Canadian casualty, only to feel relief—and guilt—when another soldier's name was announced. Nonetheless, we still spent his first tour in a near-permanent state of anxiety. I watched the channel 11 news obsessively, three times a day, wondering if I knew the latest fallen soldier.

At the time, I was a very new mother to a baby girl, and, still overwhelmed by my astonishing and surely unique ability to create life, I was even more appalled than usual at the thought of the violent premature ending of it. Mum and Dad seemed outwardly calm and resigned, but there was a sense of strain about them. Our tension built over days of watching upsetting reports on television; relief would come with a phone call from Dave and would last a day or so before the fear started once again to grow. We were all on edge, for eight long months.

In August of 2006, Dave returned home from Afghanistan. And then, four years later, he went back.

• • •

Apart from two brief leaves home, my brother has been absent for most of his extended 2010–11 tour. We do of course miss him; we look forward to his phone calls and emails from that dusty, distant and impossibly foreign country. But it's odd that this time, life without him has become as commonplace as having him nearby. For one thing, Dave lives in Squamish, almost an hour from me, so we don't see him most days. As well, while there is a symbolic empty seat at Mum and Dad's dining table at family gatherings, and regret that he will not make it home to help decorate the Christmas tree or blow out his birthday candles, during this trip I haven't sensed a brother-shaped hole in the house that everyone is trying to ignore. He's at work, and he'll be back later, and until then we'll just carry on as usual. I lived abroad myself, for nearly 10 years; I suppose everyone at home felt the same about me.

Frequently, family conversations about Dave are theoretical rather than factual. Though he calls often, security issues usually prevent him from telling us much—or, indeed, anything—about what he has been doing. So instead of having a vivid mental picture of him at war, in his fatigues, directing his troops, at these times I instead imagine Dave sitting quietly by himself in a darkened compound in the middle of southern Afghanistan, eating a delicious meal. I see him having rice, and possibly roast lamb, and there may be saffron and cinnamon and apricots—all ingredients from a supper he cooked for us after returning from his first tour. (The meals there are apparently always delicious, and unlike details of his day-to-day operations, they're never classified.)

These large gaps in our understanding are familiar, as there were plenty of similar silences in 2006; back then, though, we had the media to fill in many gaps for us that Dave could not. The reports on the television were often bad, but at least there was news of the mission. These days, now that deaths of Canadian soldiers are rare, I occasionally see reports of village elders welcoming NATO engineers, and Kabul men being sworn in as police recruits, but stories from Afghanistan are less common. To the media, good news is no news.

• • •

During Dave's 2006 tour, my family all sported our Canadian Forces–sponsored yellow ribbon pins—on our cars, in our windows and on my baby stroller. (Mum also tied long yellow ribbons to her cherry trees at home.) There were very few of them around at the time, in Vancouver, and I noted then how strange it was that no one asked me what they were for. Perhaps people thought the ribbons represented a cancer charity or another more universally acknowledged good cause.

I also suspected that my liberal, urban West Coast friends were hesitant to acknowledge such a blatant symbol in support of soldiers fighting a conflict that so many opposed—I wore that ribbon everywhere, yet none of my media-savvy pals ever commented on it. As

Canada's role in this conflict shrinks, I think such attitudes are mellowing. Our soldiers are—mostly—coming home, and the ones who do stay won't be fighting anymore. Training and education will continue, but these are efforts most people support.

It's been amusing, exasperating and enlightening to note people's reactions to the phrase, "My brother is serving in Afghanistan"—reactions that have barely changed in the past four years. To start, faces freeze in a polite smile, perhaps to hide surprise or shock, and I always wonder if we aren't the right sort of family to have a serving soldier in our midst. Then, after the initial "Oh!" there's a pause while they search for the correct thing to say. Have there been many successes lately? What about casualties? Are we winning? Do girls get to go to school now?

There are occasionally more puzzling comments. "Well, I'm a pacifist!" said one woman to me, brightly. Well—great! Good for you! As it happens, I told her, probably every single person in every family of a serving member of the Forces stationed in Afghanistan is a pacifist, too. And then there was the man who listed in detail for me the reasons why he would have refused to go to Afghanistan if he was a member of the army, and that they would have had to imprison him for desertion, and then finished by saying that of course he would never join the Forces in the first place.

Mostly, they ask questions; many do not share their opinions. And to me at least, there's no wrong thing to say. I have a number of thoughts about the conflict, many of them at odds with each other. I don't know if we should have taken part in the first place and am dubious about the reasons that were given at the time. I'm not sure if the current Afghan government is any better for its people than the Taliban was, and I doubt the myriad problems of Afghanistan can ever be "fixed" by outsiders.

I don't know if we should even try. Closer to home, I am torn by the casual acceptance of injury, disability and death as understandable consequences of choosing a career in the Armed Forces—not just by members of the public, but by Forces personnel themselves.

What others might think of this cause makes no difference to Dave's commitment to it; he would go there regardless, as would so many of his colleagues. On the one hand, this makes me proud of him. On the other, it unsettles me. As a mother now to two young children—both of whom think Uncle Dave is a neat guy to have around for pillow fights, and who also sometimes wears strange outfits and goes away on long trips—it's painful to imagine having so little control over their lives that I could not keep them from putting themselves inside a war zone.

This devotion to duty puts those of us on the home front in a strange and often uncomfortable position when we find ourselves in conversations about Canada's NATO role. People without our emotional ties to the mission can easily articulate their feelings about it, but my personal connection to the mission, combined with my ambivalence about it, sometimes leaves me wondering what side I am on. I can tie yellow ribbons and send care packages, and then feel guilty and disloyal when I wonder: what's the point? Why is Canada involved in this? I am pleased when people are concerned and ask about Dave's safety. But I also don't mind if they ask why he has been put in the line of fire—or has put himself there—for dubious presidential legacies, elaborate international conspiracies or nefarious foreign oil cartels.

People ask what Dave does "over there," or what his rank is. (He's a major.) But I don't move in military circles, and most of my friends have no idea what life in the Forces is like—neither do I. Even if people aren't political, there's a whiff of neo-conservatism about the whole subject that makes many Vancouverites nervous. And so they usually end the discussion with a big sigh, a neutral comment about his safe return and a change of subject.

• • •

My big brother will shortly come home from Afghanistan. After a few weeks, Dave will settle back into normal life; he will no longer have centre stage at all family gatherings, and we'll go back to discussing the weather, hockey and politics. But even though we won't talk about it most of the time, there will still be a part of him over there. And I'll still freeze, briefly, if I hear of a soldier lost in Kandahar, even though there is no chance it will be my soldier anymore.

A few days ago I was driving outside of Vancouver, in a rural area full of cows and wide grassy fields bordered by hills and sky. For a confirmed and contented city dweller like me, this felt like foreign territory. But suddenly I passed a mailbox—at the foot of a driveway so long that the house it belonged to was nowhere to be seen—with two Canadian flags attached, and two small yellow ribbons tied in bows, flapping in the breeze.

I know nothing about that family. But just like a Canadian traveller spotting a maple leaf on a backpack in deepest Siberia, I knew instantly those yellow ribbons meant that they and I were in the same club. We never wanted to join it, and we'll be happy when we're no longer members. But for now, we're not alone.

IN ONE OF THE STARS I SHALL BE LIVING

(An excerpt from *For Your Tomorrow*)

Melanie Murray

July 1, 2007. The fireworks explode in a fountain of light—flamingo, orange, purple, gold—and fade into the darkness. They're cascading over Okanagan Lake, several kilometres away. But we can see them from the deck, through the leafy branches of the walnut tree.

"Happy Canada Day!" I raise my glass to Mica, sitting across the table from me. She and her partner, Aaron, arrived in Kelowna yesterday; they drove down from Yellowknife after completing a three-year teaching stint at the First Nations community of Rae-Edzo on Great Slave Lake. We clink our glasses. "Ah … St. Hubertus Gewürztraminer. The grapes grow on the hillside just a few kilometres from here," I say, swirling and sniffing. "Lychee and melon on the nose."

"A hint of rose petal too," Mica laughs at our oenophile charade, reminding me so much of her mother, my sister, at 30 years old—dimpled chin, freckles, long dark hair. "And here's to Jeff. To his safe return . . . in just a few weeks." She smiles, the diamond stud in her nose glinting in the candlelight. Her brother, Jeff, is serving in Afghanistan with the Canadian military. When I ask how she's coped with the anxiety of having her brother in a war zone for the past five months, she confesses her vulnerability. "I haven't told many people about him being in Afghanistan. On Easter Sunday, the day the six Canadian soldiers were killed, I really crumbled. We didn't hear their names for hours after it was first broadcast."

Three more soldiers killed just last week by another IED. I shake my head.

When Jeff was home for his mid-deployment leave in April, Mica got four days off and flew back to Halifax to be with him and their family. "He made us feel so confident about his safety," she says, her eyes brightening. "He said he'll be staying in the same secure outpost—they call it 'the Hotel'—until he returns in mid-August."

The spicy scent of walnut leaves wafts in the warm breeze. We sip our wine and talk about their trip to Vancouver Island the day after tomorrow. They will meet up with friends to hike the West Coast Trail, one of the most gruelling treks in North America. For 75 kilometres, it follows a rugged shoreline of spectacular ocean vistas, tidal pools, marine caves and the tallest trees in Canada. Then they'll drive their packed-to-the-rooftop black Hyundai back home to Nova Scotia.

Their camping gear clutters the lawn below the deck—tent, sleeping bags, foamies, headlamps, rain jackets, camp stove. Under the lights, Aaron attempts to organize it into their backpacks. "I don't know, Mica," he calls up, "either half of your clothes stay behind, or we won't be taking much food."

"We can eat salmonberries," she chuckles. "Melanie's been telling me that the bushes along the trail are full of them."

"Yeah, and we'll dig for clams, steam them over a driftwood fire—go native," he grins up at us. "No need to pack food."

Like two kids let loose for the summer, they exude the carefree excitement that comes with being on the road—your hours and days defined by a map of Canada spread out before you.

• • •

July 4, 2007. The explosion reverberates across Iran, Iraq and Syria; rumbles under the seas of the azure Mediterranean; resounds over the wind-blown deserts of North Africa; rolls over the waves of the blue-grey Atlantic, and crashes onto the rockbound shores of eastern Canada.

• • •

"Get those guys out of there! Get them off the ground!" I shouted at the radio when the news announced the deaths of six Canadian soldiers in Afghanistan. By 10 that morning, the identities of four of them were confirmed.

Now, waiting for the next report, I dwell in a limbo of fear, a refrain replaying in my mind: this couldn't happen to Jeff . . . to my sister . . . we've already sacrificed one of our men, our father, to the maw of the military. Faced with the randomness of roadside bombs, Jeff has survived so far. In only four weeks, he'll be home—home to begin a whole new phase of his life, as a father to his beautiful son, born just 10 weeks before he left for Afghanistan. When he comes back in August, he'll be posted to Toronto, where Sylvie works for Air Canada. They'll begin their life together as a family. The map of his future is laid out, just waiting for him to return and step into it.

I try to stave off my trepidation, glad I have my packing to keep me occupied. On this sweltering July morning, I'm in a flurry of washing clothes and organizing suitcases for our trip to Halifax tomorrow. My younger son, Gabriel, and I will spend six weeks in the Maritimes, escape the motorized whirr of the Kelowna suburbs—the lawn mowers, weed whackers, leaf blowers, power washers, hedge trimmers—trade it all for the rushing waves of the Northumberland Strait and the undulating call of the loons at my sisters' cottage on Grand Lake.

Just before 11 o'clock, the phone rings. The voice on the line sounds at once familiar and strange. "Melanie, it's Russ," a timorous tone I've never heard from my gregarious brother-in-law. Is something wrong? He must be calling about picking us up at the airport tomorrow.

"Jeff was one of the soldiers killed this morning."

It's as if I've been jolted with thousands of volts of electrical current. Stunned and numbed, I can't move, or speak. Not Jeff . . . please . . . not Jeff.

"No!" I want him to take back the words. This can't be possible. In the background, I hear my sister moaning, keening for her son. I need to be there, to hold her.

A former military man himself, Russ can summon the focus of his logistician's mind, to override the turmoil of the distraught father. "Melanie," he says in a controlled, level voice, "do you know how we can get in touch with Mica?"

My god, dear Mica.

Today they begin their trek of the West Coast Trail. Once they're en route, they'll be in total isolation. But Mica said they would first have an orientation session at the trailhead. "Maybe we can reach them at the parks office before they set out," I say, trying to reassure Russ. I know how much they need their daughter right now, their only living child. "I'll try to track her down."

I'm amazed at the clarity of mind that can surface in the turmoil of crisis, surely a survival mechanism. In my shaking and distress, I can find the phone book, locate the right section at the back—Government of Canada—and the Parks Department number, punch the digits into the phone, explain the urgency of contacting my niece and finally reach the West Coast Trail Hiker Registration office at the Gordon River Trailhead. "Let's see . . . yeah, Mica Francis is registered to begin hiking today," says a pleasant voice. "In fact, she just had her orientation. She left about 10 minutes ago to take the ferry to the trail."

"There's a family emergency. Mica has to call home as soon as possible." My tone is sufficiently panicked that a park warden is immediately dispatched to catch the boat before it leaves. "Please call me back to let me know if Mica gets this message," I say before hanging up. I imagine Mica, her dark hair tied back in a ponytail, her hazel eyes shining with excitement, sitting with her backpack in a boat on the edge of the Pacific, about to embark on an adventure.

• • •

My Siamese cross bathes in a pool of sunlight on the birch floor. He licks his white paws, swabs his ears, licks and swabs, over and over—as if nothing has changed. I glare at the black phone, and visualize Mica making the call home. The dam of emotion bursts, releases a flood of tears and pent-up anger: "Jesus fucking Christ!" I scream into the indifferent air. "Why are they driving around in the desert when any second they could be blown up? It's a fucking game of Russian roulette!"

I respect my nephew's dedication to helping a suffering people, but I'm not a supporter of our military's mission in Afghanistan. Considering the country's 30-year history of war, the corruption inherent in Afghan tribal politics, its police force and the government itself, I doubt that long-term progress is achievable. And with each Canadian soldier who's killed, I become more vehemently opposed to our military presence there. Most of the deaths are from roadside bombs. Why aren't helicopters being used to transport our troops? Is our military adequately equipped for combat? And now Jeff—my intelligent, brave and gentle nephew—has been struck down in the prime of his life, one more sacrifice to the god of war.

The ringing phone disrupts my crying rage. I seize the receiver, praying it's the hikers' registration office to tell me they've located my niece. But the lilting voice on the line is Mica's, higher pitched than usual, a voice that's trying to stay composed. She's not been told to call home, but to call me. The shock waves reverberate over the phone lines to an island on the edge of the Pacific. "Mica," I say, attempting equanimity, "you need to phone home right away."

"Is something wrong? Is it Jeff?"

"Mica . . . I don't want to tell you this."

"Is he dead?"

My lips move, but the words won't come out. Long seconds of silence before I can say, "Mica . . . I'm so sorry to have to tell you this. Yes."

"Oh god," she cries. "What happened?"

"A roadside bomb."

"Jeff," her voice trembles. "Just like the others."

"You'd better call home now, Mica. I'll be there soon."

"Okay, Melanie," she says, stifling her sobs, "thank you."

• • •

Atop the Peace Tower on Parliament Hill, a red-and-white flag flaps crisply against a clear cerulean sky. But in the offices of the Gothic revival sandstone buildings, chaos reigns. It's one of the darkest days in the four-year Canadian military mission in Afghanistan, the worst since Easter Sunday. Just down the street on Colonel By Drive, in the concrete block towers of the National Defence Headquarters, military officials issue press releases, determine next of kin and confirm phone numbers and addresses. They assign notification teams to knock on the doors of each of the six soldiers' families.

From coast to coast, in pods of three—a senior officer from the base, an assisting officer and a padre—they travel: to homes in Iqaluit, Nunavut; Burnaby, British Columbia; Whitecourt, Alberta; Clearwater, Manitoba; Ottawa and Kingston, Ontario; and Eastern Passage, Nova Scotia. They walk up to the doors of the parents who made him, nested and nurtured him until he could fly on his own; up to the doors of wives-in-waiting, each one crossing off the days on the calendar—just four more weeks!—until her beloved lies beside her in the long night; up to the doors of children who'll never again see their father's eyes beam love into theirs, never again snuggle into the shelter of his strong arms.

• • •

July 6. In the murk of early morning, I lie in Jeff's bed, sleepless. Stars glow on the ceiling above me—the constellation of Scorpio that Jeff put up there a couple of years ago.

One morning during the Christmas holidays, he came into the kitchen to show his mother the glow-in-the-dark stars he'd just bought. He stood on a bar stool and placed one large star over the wooden island where she was chopping vegetables. "This one's for you, Mom," he said. Then he went upstairs and positioned the stars on his bedroom ceiling: five stars in the outstretched claws, a string of six stars in the body, and five to form the smooth bend of the stinging tail—a horizontal outline of the letter J. He called down to his mother to come up and see his star chart. A map, the place to find him. "In one of the stars I shall be living," says the Little Prince in one of Jeff's favourite books—there on his bookshelf, an arm's length from the bed.

I arrived in Eastern Passage late last night. Marion and Russ were already in bed, exhausted from facing the impossible new reality of their lives, the details of their son's death springing up through the day like noxious weeds. When I stepped into Jeff's room, I was engulfed by his presence—but at the same time, confronted with his irrevocable absence. His khaki cargo pants hung limply on a hook behind the door. His framed photos looked at me from the top of the cherry wood dresser: Jeff, a teenager, embraces his granny; Sylvie encircled by his arms, he in an orange polo shirt, she in an orange sweater—their first date, carving pumpkins; and the young man, a few months ago—a proud father holding his infant son. In the centre of the images, a brass statue of a seated Buddha; on the wall above, the framed Second World War service certificate bearing his grandfather's picture.

Then my eyes moved to the titles in his overflowing bookcase. I shook my head, awed by the breadth, depth and eclecticism of his learning and intellect: several titles by his philosophical guru, Michel Foucault (*Society Must Be Defended, Ethics: Subjectivity and Truth* and

Discipline and Punish: The Birth of the Prison); many on military history and strategy (Gwynne Dyer's *War* and *Ignorant Armies: Sliding into War in Iraq*, Michael Ignatieff's *Virtual War*, John Keegan's *A History of Warfare* and *Intelligence in War*); myriad martial arts titles (*Unleash the Warrior Within, Bushido: The Way of the Warrior, Budo Secrets: Teachings of the Martial Arts Masters*); numerous books on Buddhism (*Cittaviveka: Teachings from the Silent Mind, The Shambhala Guide to Aikido: The Way of Peace, Shambhala: The Sacred Path of the Warrior*); and two books by mythologist Joseph Campbell (*The Hero with a Thousand Faces* and *The Power of Myth*).

I pulled out Campbell's texts and flipped through their pages, replete with Jeff's annotations and yellow highlighting of passages:

> The hero is someone who has given his life to something bigger than himself. Freud, Jung, and their followers have demonstrated irrefutably, that the logic, the heroes, and the deeds of myth survive into modern times. Herohood is pre-destined rather than simply achieved.

Was this another map, I wondered, another place to find him? During my flight from Kelowna to Halifax, suspended 37,000 feet in space, I had contemplated the arc of Jeff's life, its similarity to the archetypal stages of the hero's journey. A glimmer of light appeared, an inkling of a pattern in the events leading up to, and culminating on, July 4—events that otherwise seemed cruelly random and senseless: Why Jeff? He had so much to live for.

Now as I lie beneath his floral comforter, a salty breeze blows through the window looking east onto the ocean and the blinking lighthouse on Devil's Island. Waves hush on the shore—the sounds and scents of Nova Scotia, my heart's home. Every summer I leave behind the tropical dry heat of the Okanagan to dwell in the misty east coast and the warmth of my family. My sister, Marion, is as close to me as anyone can be. One year older, she was always there to play with, and watch over me, during our early childhood in Malagash. In the early seventies, when I was an undergraduate at the University of New Brunswick, Marion, Russ and three-year-old Jeff lived one floor below me in the Park Hill apartments overlooking the Saint John River. Some days, I'd hear a faint knocking and unlock the door to see my freckle-faced nephew smiling up at me. He would toddle down the red-carpeted corridor to the stairwell, mount the cement stairs to the second floor, pull open the heavy fire door and find my apartment—by himself. A few minutes later, I'd be opening the cookie tin when the phone would ring. "Is he there yet?" Marion would ask, and laugh with relief.

Last November, I joined in her exultation when her grandson—Jeff's son—was born, the primogeniture of our family's next generation. And in the past five months, I've commiserated in her all-consuming worry while Jeff was in Afghanistan.

Now, I must descend with her into the hell of our most fearful nightmare—one of our children dying before we do.

I wake to the smell of coffee and a sound like the soft cooing of doves—the murmuring of a contented baby. I go downstairs to the kitchen. Marion stands in the sunlit window, holding her grandson. For the first time, I see my sister as a grandmother, proudly embracing her treasure; and see her for the first time as a mother-in-mourning, grief already etching its fine lines in her face, darkly circling her eyes. And I behold for the very first time the bluest eyes, the rosiest chubby cheeks, the heart-shaped face and dimpled chin of Jeff's baby son, made in the image of his father.

I smile, for the blessing of this beautiful child; at the same time I cry, for his father's eternal absence and my sister's loss. I put my arms around them. "I am so broken . . ." Marion whispers. We look into each other's eyes. I can feel it in her body, so fragile it could crumble in my arms. I hear it in her voice, cracked and dry. I see it in her brown eyes, brimming with tears. "How is this possible?" she shakes her head. "Before he left, I asked Jeff if he knew what it would do to us if anything happened to him."

"And what did he say?"

"He said nothing would happen to him—that he'd be okay."

Did he really believe this? Could he have gone unless he believed this? Jeff was no raw young recruit, harbouring youthful delusions of invulnerability. He joined the military at 30, after a decade of university studies. He embarked on the Afghanistan mission as a mature, thoughtful man. Was his response to his mother's question meant to quell her fears as he headed off to a war zone on the other side of the world? Was he, like all soldiers, playing the odds in God's lottery—that significantly more would survive than be killed, that he wouldn't be one of the unlucky ones?

Before he left for Afghanistan, Jeff must have looked death in the face. Forty-two of his comrades had already been killed—one a friend from his regiment, Nichola Goddard, also a forward observation officer. Like every deployed soldier, Jeff had to ensure that his legal affairs were in order, had to choose a photograph to be issued to the media in the event of his death. He posed in his dark green uniform in front of the Canadian flag, knowing there would be only one reason that his family would ever see this picture—enlarged to a 24-by-36-inch framed colour portrait and delivered to his grief-stricken family. When you see these photos of our soldiers in the media, you'll notice that none of them are smiling.

This picture isn't the one Jeff chose to be released in the event of his death. Rather, he selected one taken in Afghanistan: He stands in front his crew's LAV—Lucky 13—dressed in his tan camouflage uniform and helmet with dust goggles attached. The desert sun lights up his face, the boyish freckles on his sunburnt nose and cheeks. His hazel eyes squint, but his gaze is direct. And he is smiling, a knowing half-smile. It's a photo that seems to say *amor fati*, love of one's fate—not fatalism, but love of the life one is called to live.

WE ARE (A MILITARY) FAMILY

Kelly Thompson

When I was little, my friends and I played house in the sand dunes that served as the training area behind Canadian Forces Base Borden. Back then, we dreamed of being veterinarians, doctors or actresses—not soldiers. Not one of my childhood friends talked of following in their parents' combat boot footsteps. But now, when I log into Facebook, I see names and faces from my youth, proudly wearing their military uniforms—just as I have done—and carrying on in the family business.

I first became aware of the extent of my family's military heritage when I was about five years old. My mother worked as a nurse, and my soldier dad was posted to Borden. Due to housing restrictions at the time, a military home wasn't available for the entire family, so my mom, sister and I lived about three hours away, and Dad came home on weekends. Although I knew Dad was in the Forces, I couldn't conceive of what it meant to be a soldier. But I did know that on Sundays, when my father's uniform came out of the closet, it meant he was returning to Borden and unwillingly leaving us behind. While we waited for housing to be made available, and before I began school, Grandpa Thompson came to look after me during the day.

Grandpa T was an infantryman who eventually became a military police officer, retiring after 20 years. But the idea of him as a young man, involved in war, was beyond my five-year-old comprehension. Every morning he would report for child-care duty, carrying a bag filled with goodies that piqued my interest. He would sit on our scratchy, plaid couch and call for his "Moo Moo," a nickname he donned on me somewhere along the way.

One day, Grandpa called me to his side and produced a book with "Korea" printed in large red letters. He opened it so I could see the browning photos inside, curling up at the edges. "This is me," he said, pointing to a skinny man in uniform with one arm steadying a large machine gun and the other arm slung around a comrade. "I was infantry," he said as he patted his chest where his medals should have been. He flipped the pages slowly, turning each one with the tip of his pointer finger, letting them fall with a soft whoosh. For a moment, I saw Grandpa as someone who had a life beyond our days of laughter, storytelling and hide-and-seek. He was once someone who shot Vickers machine guns and smoked thin, brown cigars that he stomped into the swamp of Korea with the toe of his mud-caked boot. Although he never spoke about it, Grandpa T saved a man during that war, pulling him out of a bomb crater and binding his horrific wounds. Grandpa was a hero.

As I grew up, I became increasingly aware of my family's military history, but up until the moment I joined, I remained staunchly against joining. Instead of military life, I wanted to write, and to me, this was something a soldier never did, except the odd report or memorandum.

I wrote my stories, edited and laminated the pages, bound them with yarn and then I would hold the volumes in my hand and be proud that I had developed a story into something tangible. I refused to write about soldiers, because they were too close to my reality, and although I couldn't possibly understand the things my father, grandfather and great-grandfather did in order to survive during their respective wars, I knew that those things haunted them. Instead, I chose to write about fantasy and figments of my imagination, because fictional things were safer and less hurtful to the ones I loved.

Once military housing was available and we were finally able to move to Borden to live with my father, I learned that this didn't necessarily mean we would see him more often. He travelled often for work, to conferences in Europe, to the other side of Canada and occasionally to the back fields of Borden on training exercises—just a few kilometres away, but completely out of reach. Dad missed many Christmases, anniversaries and birthdays, but this is part of the sacrifice of military life. It is a sacrifice that both the soldier and the family must make.

When he was not away, I would sit on the porch stairs, waiting for him to return from work at the end of the day, and then follow him through his ritualistic transformation. I watched as he arrived, stepping out of the car with his combat boots already unlaced. He would stand in the foyer and methodically unbutton his camouflage shirt as he stepped out of his boots. He then made his way up the stairs, where he would drape the shirt over the back of the chair in the office, and the boots would be placed rigidly underneath the seat. He would stroll into the bedroom and I would wait outside, telling him about my day through the double doors, as the jeans came out of the closet and were pulled over white legs that no longer had hair on the calves (the combat boots having long since rubbed it all away). I relished the process of my father being transformed into a civilian. The routine of it was extremely comforting.

My dad gave his entire working life to the Forces, serving for over 35 years, first as a vehicle technician and later as an officer. He enrolled as a private but retired as a major—quite the achievement in the military business. Dad led his troops with courage and dedication that I admired when I was young and then respected even more when I became an officer myself. He wanted nothing more than to serve and joined as soon as he was legally old enough. But for me, I couldn't imagine myself entrenched further in military life and it was never expected of me.

Dad did two tours to the Golan in the 1970s and admits that he was forever changed after witnessing the atrocities of war. Maybe, without that war, he would have been more laid-back about curfew or less militant in his assigning of the household chores during the family "O Group," which I later learned is army slang for Orders Group. (Most regular folk call them family meetings.) Or maybe his actions as a father were as much a result of his training as of the inevitable products of his war experiences. As children, my sister and I knew that there were certain things we couldn't do with Dad. We were not allowed to wake him up when he was sleeping, unless we called out from across the room, as he often woke startled and flailing, regaining composure moments later when he realized he was not in the desert but rather on his own living room couch. We could never ask questions about what Dad had done when he was overseas. It was only at the end of his career that my father finally began to acknowledge the things he had been forced to see and do, and the ramifications of those actions on his emotions. Just as I was joining the Forces, I began to see changes in my dad: he was quicker to anger and have other emotional outbursts, and he gradually began to withdraw from his troops and his family. But when he had his uniform on, my father remained the consummate professional. His salute was straighter than any I have ever seen and his uniform consistently immaculate.

Although my dad spent the majority of his career moving every few years, by the time I was heading into high school he had managed to shift between different jobs within CFB Borden, so I was able to go to the same school for the whole four years. Until then, I had spent my entire childhood at schools on bases, where every student's parents were also military members. I never kept friends for longer than a few years, because their families were also consistently posted elsewhere, never to be heard from again, despite pen pal attempts. So when it came time for high school, it was daunting to stroll into an off-base school as the "newbie" in a town like Alliston, Ontario, where everyone has known each other since birth. The farming town residents exuded a consistency that I craved. Their friends and family members all lived nearby, and on holidays no one was ever missing from their dinner table. That craving for stability only furthered my determination that I would never be a soldier.

• • •

Grandpa T died a year before September 11, 2001, when I was just 16. His death and the day that the Twin Towers went down were the catalysts for my eventual decision to enrol in the military. My friends and I watched the terrorist attacks on a television that had been pushed into our Grade 12 English classroom. I was horrified, as we all were, but unlike my classmates of the sleepy town, I was also thinking of what this act of terrorism would mean for my father and for our military.

A short while later, I walked into the recruitment centre to start the long application process. My friends were shocked and couldn't fathom that their artsy, wild-haired and carefree friend was signing up to carry a weapon and potentially go to war. For a while, I allowed their muffled laughter to make me question my decision, but my parents assured me that if I wanted to be in the military badly enough, I would succeed.

There were many reasons that propelled me to join the Forces. Yes, I joined because I wanted to serve my country like Grandpa T as we headed into a time of extreme uncertainty, but I also joined to pay for my education—in my case, a professional writing degree that wasn't just a dream but a passion. I joined because the military was what I knew, and most of all because I craved a deeper connection with my military family. I realized that when I was five years old and Grandpa T first introduced me to the notion of military life, I felt pride in my family and the sacrifices that they made. My great-grandfathers, grandfathers and father had all signed up when the nation had expected it of them, and despite my vow not to, I eventually did the same.

Before heading off to St. Jean, Quebec, for an arduous 10 weeks of training, there was a series of tests that I had to pass. I completed my medical and then sweated through the physical training test. I did a two-hour-long aptitude exam and sat through a three-hour interview, answering questions about the imaginary decisions I might make as an officer. It was all a little surreal. After the paperwork was signed and filed away, I was shipped off to basic training, and it would be a lie to say I had an easy time of it. I was 18, and it was my first time away from home. Suddenly, I was living a province away from my family, someone was yelling at me every day, and every insecurity that I had ever harboured was now being thrown in my face and used to break me into the soldier mentality. At night I would reach into my pocket to feel for the small notepad and pen, pull them out and write about my day: the challenges, the bruises and my desperation for home.

During a particularly gruelling obstacle course run, we were ordered to make our best "angry soldier noises" as we crossed the final obstacle—a rather unstable rope bridge. It seemed an odd request, but we weren't a group allowed to argue. When I got to the other side of the bridge, fresh from my "angry noise" experience, my sergeant yelled out, "THOMPSON! What the hell was that?! I said sound ANGRY!" I thought I had sounded furious enough, but apparently not. So I redid the obstacle course, with my entire platoon watching, and screamed my heart out as the rope bridge wobbled underneath me. When I collapsed next to my platoon mates, embarrassed, sweating, exhausted and now legitimately angry, I thought to myself, how the hell did I get here?

Eventually, I fell into the routine of waking up at 4:30 AM to shine my shoes and run for 10 kilometres. And in a strange way, I even started to like it. It was all going smoothly—until I broke my leg from carrying too much weight during an extended rucksack march. I adopted the mentality engrained in me and "soldiered on" when my sergeant directed me to. I slung my 70-pound rucksack on my back and continued to march 20 kilometres a day for the rest of the week. With the help of an endless supply of ice and ibuprofen, I managed to get through it.

When it was all over, my parents came down for my graduation parade. Dad marvelled at my blistered feet, painfully swollen leg and un-manicured hands, which were grubby with stubborn dirt, and I don't know if he had ever looked at me with more pride. Maybe that's the day that I officially became a Thompson. My basic training graduation was my dad's last day in uniform before he retired, and after his lifetime of service, he could now officially pass the torch to me. The military had been his whole life. When he finally retired, it became clear that without the rigid routine that the military provided, Dad struggled.

For a long time, mental health injuries were either ignored or dismissed in the military. There was no training for the families about how to cope with the return of a loved one who had become a stranger. There was no psychological assistance for those who returned from war and no discourse about improvement of services. For too long, we have taught our soldiers to "suck it up and soldier on," whether the pain is physical or mental, the latter being a stigma that many military members cannot bear. I have "soldiered on" just like the other Thompson generations. But I'd like to think that after the war in Afghanistan, our country is acknowledging that soldiers need support and systems to heal their visible and invisible wounds. We have a long way to go, but we're getting there.

I discovered that the same stigma exists in military families; mental health injuries were not spoken of. It wasn't until my grandfather was in the hospital, his life slipping away from him, that my dad says they spoke about their wartime experiences—a conversation they both waited to have their entire lives, because only someone else who has lived it can ever understand it. And as it turns out, it wasn't until my father and I had both ended our military careers that we were finally able to discuss our experiences in the Forces and how they had changed us.

• • •

Once I finished university, I was posted to my first unit, handed a platoon full of subordinates and told to run things, despite being only 21 years old. In my eight-year military career, I saw nothing of combat or life overseas due to my broken leg, which never properly healed. The appropriate and brave soldier statement would be to say that I wanted to go, but it would be a lie. Admitting that, as a soldier, is no easy feat. I was worried that I would come home scarred and angry, like so many of my comrades and family. As someone who can't even pass a stray dog on the street without crying, I worried that a tour in a war zone would shake me to my core.

Yes, for the most part, my career has been spent at a desk, filling out paperwork and supporting those who were deploying and leaving their loved ones for a long six months. In place of overseas tours, I have my broken leg as my eternal mark of service. The permanent limp is my "war wound"—proof that I served my country. My entire career has been spent on the home front, but I find no shame in that.

Although my military career might seem mundane to some, it has been shockingly fulfilling. I travelled the world, I served with the security force in Vancouver during the 2010 Olympics and I worked alongside some incredible troops. The military has taught me that I am more capable than I imagined, and that I can challenge my own ideas of what I think is possible. I have made lifelong friends who've shared this crazy military life with me. But I have also relived the lives of my father and grandfather, constantly travelling and leaving loved ones behind. I spent endless days away from home, either on courses, on exercises or on taskings. I travelled so much that at the end of one particularly exhausting year, I calculated that I had actually been in my own bed for a total of only two months. It's not a life that lends to easy maintenance of relationships on the home front.

· · ·

My leg, and its refusal to heal, has meant that September 11, 2011, was my last day in the military. I was medically released from the Forces, just eight short years after I joined—strangely and exactly 10 years after one of the catalysts for my enrolment. I am slowly making the transition into a civilian life I know nothing about—the same transition that all four generations of my family have gone through before me—exchanging a uniform for jeans and learning to stop calling people "Sir."

The day before I handed in my uniforms, my dad and I rifled through my kit bags and pulled out different pieces of gear, talked about how certain pieces had improved over the years and threw a few acronyms around, using our military secret language. As my release date grew nearer, I clung to that military bond with my father more than ever. The military is like a club, and once you hand in your ID card and your uniforms, suddenly you've lost your membership. When the day came, I gathered up my gear to be taken to the clothing depot, where it would be assigned to another soldier to wear. I closed my eyes, took in a deep breath and could still smell the fields of Farnham, where my career began. I unfolded my mattress roll to make sure all the air was released, and came across my name and service number, emblazoned like a tattoo that once identified me as a soldier—and then I left it all behind. When I walked out of the depot, releasing my military identity, I had a moment of panic. What if I didn't know how to function as a civilian? I got into my car, started the ignition and cried, both for the career that I lost and for the unfamiliar future that scared me.

• • •

On a bookcase in my parents' home, there is a photo of every military member who has graced our family. There is my mother's father, in his sleek navy uniform, smiling youthfully into the frame. There is my father, in his army greens, a stern look on his face and a Canada flag waving behind him. There is my favourite photo of Grandpa T, a grainy black-and-white image taken before he got on the ship to Korea. And then there is my first military portrait. I am the only soldier on the bookcase who wears air force blue, and I hold my head with pride, my sword at a 90-degree angle, sweat gleaming on my forehead in the stifling July heat. My white belt and gloves had been scrubbed thoroughly in the sink the night before and my hair is pulled back into the perfectly polished bun that the military demands of its female employees. I was only 18, but at the time I felt very grown up and proud to be carrying on the Thompson tradition.

At 27 years old, I am now considered a veteran. Somehow, despite my fears and without the bizarre safety net of the military life, I know I can create an identity that goes beyond that of soldier and veteran. I am a writer, an in-the-shower singer, a best friend, an animal lover and a daughter. So much of my future is yet to be written.

FALLING FOR A SOLDIER: THE BATTLE LINES OF A LOVE TRIANGLE

Shaun Hunter

When you let a stranger into your basement, you never know what will snag their attention. The young man from the city water services department was staring at two dark-green metal containers on the bottom shelf of the pantry: ammo boxes. I hurried to explain that they were filled with shoe polish, but he had already formed his conclusion.

"So, you were in the army."

"Not me. My husband."

His remark startled me. It had been almost 30 years since I'd battled a Canadian Forces reserve regiment for my husband's loyalty; I thought I'd done a better job burying the evidence of that long-ago love triangle.

When Blair and I met in a lineup at the University of Toronto in the fall of 1982, I had no idea a suitor was already vying for his affections. Blair was a history and economics student recruiting for the debate club; I was new to U of T, on exchange from a women's college in Massachusetts, where I was studying English literature. We talked for fewer than five minutes, but I found out enough to know I wasn't interested in the debate club or its recruiter. Like me, Blair had grown up in Calgary, a city from which I'd done my best to escape. He was a debater—the over-confident, know-it-all type I'd hoped to avoid by going to a women's college. And then there was the moustache. Later, after he'd coaxed my phone number from me, I found out Blair's facial hair was army issue. A moustache, he explained, was one of the few ways a male soldier could assert his individuality.

I couldn't understand why an intelligent person would surrender himself to the conformity of the army. As far as I could tell, guys my age who joined up were either misfits with acne and limited social skills, or do-gooders as anachronistic and earnest as the Mormon missionaries who showed up at the door at dinnertime. As I got to know Blair, my objections crumbled. Our shared reference points in the West were refreshing, and his debate-club persona made for intrepid discussions. He had eclectic interests, a quick mind and an insatiable curiosity. By mid-term, I was starting to see past the moustache, but my concern about Blair's military involvement remained a significant obstacle: I had not come to university to fall for a soldier and get ensnared in the military subculture. As I walked to classes under the archway of the Soldiers' Tower, I felt like a hypocrite. How could I respect my relatives for the roles they had played in the Second World War, but not Blair's decision to be a volunteer soldier in a peacetime army?

Unlike my parents' wartime childhood in the 1940s, the Cold War of my youth seemed like a make-believe war, as fictional as the cartoons I watched on Saturday morning. In the sixties, the imminent threat of nuclear war was in the background of suburban Canadian life. As a child, I was curious about the tall metal tower in the field near our house—a public address system, my mother explained, in case of emergency. She didn't go into detail about what those emergencies might be, but I imagined the voice coming over the loudspeaker would sound just like the school principal when he calmly instructed us to gather in the school gym. My father showed me the jet trails left by American bombers patrolling the skies high above our house. To my child's eyes, those puffy white streaks were as pretty and harmless as clouds. I was too young to know much about Vietnam. By the time I was a teenager in the seventies, the peace symbol was already passé, something I painted on my cheeks when I dressed up as a hippie at Halloween, and protest was arguing with my mother about wearing jeans to school. The news of tanks rolling down the streets of Montreal in the fall of 1970 upset my parents, but to me the images on the television news were from another country.

Much of what I knew about soldiers came from popular culture— *Hogan's Heroes*, *M*A*S*H*, *Beetle Bailey* and *Dr. Strangelove*. If you were one of the good guys, you used the military for target practice, taking shots to get laughs. If television and movies portrayed the troops on our side as ridiculous, my Social Studies teachers made sure we learned about the gravity of war. After reading Anne Frank's diary, I took the clear, indelible message: war is evil. As a university student, my anti-military views hardened. I peppered Blair with questions and accusations. I heard his reasons for joining up—his passion for military history, his desire to test his physical and mental limits, his need to pay for university—but I didn't listen.

"Admit it. You're just learning how to kill people. Which is fucking scary." I couldn't get the stark, harrowing images in the film *Hiroshima, Mon Amour* out of my head, nor could I forget Timothy Findley's novel, *The Wars*, mired in the horrors of the First World War.

"How does war ever stop if smart people keep joining the army?"

"It's not that simple." Our conversations about the military always ended like this: me waving my objections in front of Blair like a red flag, and him telling me it wasn't that simple. My hackles went up when he tried to change the subject, but I knew that given enough time, I would win him over to my way of seeing.

• • •

A week before Remembrance Day, my phone rang.

"I was wondering if you'd accompany me to a ball."

"You mean a Cinderella kind of ball?" I imagined my American friend Lynn shushing me for my sarcasm. A nice guy asks you on a date and you're going to turn him down because he happens to be in the army? Are you crazy? She swooned over her Air Force Academy boyfriend back home in Colorado. Her dorm room walls were covered with snapshots of the two of them: Greg in his dress uniform, and Lynn a shiny bauble on his arm. I couldn't tell if my friend was more in love with the man or his aura of military prestige.

"It's the St. Andrew's Ball," Blair explained. "The regiment puts it on every year at the end of November. Scottish stuff. Kilts and bagpipes. We can take dance lessons at the armouries before the ball."

My mind raced. I wasn't like Lynn. I told Blair I'd have to think about it.

• • •

On Remembrance Day weekend, I looked out the dormer window of my residence room toward Queen's Park and the cenotaph where Blair's regiment, the 48th Highlanders, would begin its parade. My Japanese–Canadian floor-mate had sneered when I mentioned I was thinking of going.

"You're not participating in that nationalist bullshit, are you?"

I didn't want to get sucked into another lecture about the moral track record of the Canadian government. I was ashamed about the internment of the Japanese during the Second World War, and I felt the prick of personal responsibility: many of my relatives had lived in British Columbia during the war, and I suspected they had either supported the government's measures or kept their mouths shut. The internment was yet another example of how war trampled the lives of the innocent and subverted the humanity of a democratic nation. I slipped out of my room and headed for the cenotaph. If my friend stopped me in the hall, I'd use nostalgia as an excuse: I hadn't been to a Remembrance Day ceremony since the ones I helped organize in the junior high school gym. Now I remembered how I'd loved those ceremonies—the solemnity, the careful choreography, the poppies we pinned above our hearts. I wasn't religious, but Remembrance Day felt holy to me.

As I walked toward the park, I knew the real reason I was going to the parade: to test my interest in the lanky, lively young man who'd asked me to the St. Andrew's Ball. At the cenotaph, I stood near the edge of the small crowd of veterans and civilians. Two large groups of kilted soldiers—70 or 80 men in total—lined up in rows on the pavement facing the granite monument. The feathers in their bushy black hats stirred in the breeze. I scanned the rows of scarlet jackets and spotted Blair standing in front of one of the groups. His face was like stone, his eyes oblivious to the crowd, and to me. The ceremony followed the pattern we'd used in junior high: speeches, Last Post, a minute of silence, Reveille, the laying of wreaths. The sensations were familiar, too. My spine tingled, and my throat thickened with emotion at the incomprehensible mix of sacrifice, tragedy and honour. I studied the faces of the soldiers: flesh-and-blood men, with girlfriends and families and futures. I couldn't fathom how they could offer themselves and the people they loved up to war.

An officer barked his command, the bagpipes wheezed then droned, and the troops began to march. I could have turned the other way, gone back to the pile of essay assignments in my room, but instead I followed the soldiers. I walked behind them as they rounded Queen's Park and the Legislature. I continued with them down the grand boulevard of University Avenue. The story of the Pied Piper nipped at the edge of my thoughts, but I pushed it aside. The sound of the bagpipes and the roll of the snare drums reverberated in my torso and raised the fine hairs on my limbs. The highland anthems tugged me forward like ancestral music—the call to battle and the lament for the dead fused together. I didn't want to return to my cubbyhole of a room and what suddenly struck me as my trivial life. I kept walking, my steps in time with the steady rhythm of the soldiers' boots. When the parade petered out at the end of the boulevard downtown, I watched Blair mill around with the other reservists. I caught his eye, then headed back to my dorm. It wasn't the moment for conversation; I wasn't sure what I would say anyway.

• • •

I found a fancy skirt and blouse on the sale rack at Holt Renfrew. I met Blair at the armouries and set about learning how to dance the Eightsome Reel, Strip the Willow and the Gay Gordons. Analyzing English poetry was child's play next to dancing the Dashing White Sergeant with two other couples. Circle to the left . . . and back. Figure eight. Advance, stamp your feet. Retire, and clap. Pass through. Circle to the left . . . Blair stepped on my feet and I fumbled the figure eight. We looked at each other and choked back laughter.

When I wasn't focusing on my feet, I took note of the other dancers— Blair's fellow officers, their wives and girlfriends. Before the lesson started, one of the senior officers had welcomed us. He talked about the regiment as if it were a family. I glanced up at the second-floor walkway that circled the armoury hall. Through a doorway was the officers' mess—a room, Blair explained, they were encouraged to treat like a second home. As I found my spot for the Eightsome Reel, I felt my giddiness ebb. Not my family, not my home.

In my memory, the St. Andrew's Ball is a swirl of sensations. The Royal York Hotel, grand and glittering. The din of the pipes and drums. The exuberant dances. The lightness of my feet and the swish of my satin skirt. The handsome soldier who held my hand and who, at the end of the night under the brick arch of my residence, leaned down and kissed me. Then, I would have rejected the notion that I had been sprinkled with the military's version of fairy dust. I wasn't falling for a soldier; I was falling for a man who happened to be a soldier. That night in the ballroom of the Royal York Hotel, the darkness of war was nowhere to be seen. I see now that, like most girls my age, I had been weaned on fairy tales and Barbie dolls. No matter how much I resisted the military and what it stood for, no matter how much I claimed to be an independent thinker, I was susceptible to my date's attractive dress uniform and the air that shimmered with chivalry and ceremony.

That winter and the following spring, I got to know a few of Blair's fellow officers and their girlfriends and wives. I felt I was different than the other women—I was a full-time university student, I didn't come from a military family or have a military job, and I wasn't part of the old Toronto society that placed a value on the regiment's historical pedigree. I was, as my friend Lynn repeatedly reminded me, hostile to the girlfriend code of playing demure and deferential. I had opinions and I liked to speak them out loud. I wasn't good at swallowing Blair's friends' chauvinistic remarks, and I bristled at their macho swagger, candy-coated with gallantry. Most of the other women in Blair's circle of army friends had perfected the art of disappearing. Time after time, I wondered how they could drift into the shadows while their soldier men hogged the spotlight. Was I the outsider or were they?

As our first summer as a couple approached, I realized the extent to which I was involved in a love triangle with the Canadian Forces. The regiment got Tuesday nights and most weekends, and nosed her way into our life the rest of the week, too. On top of Blair's full academic load, he had boots to polish, shirts to iron and a clipboard full of matters, paltry and pressing, which required an officer's constant attention. By the time classes ended that spring, I found out the summer would be the regiment's, too: Blair was heading to Gagetown, New Brunswick, for three months of officer training. The morning of his departure, he called to say goodbye. He was racing, a thousand things to do before his flight left that night. I insisted on seeing him—just an hour, I implored—and he relented. On the restaurant patio, we sat in strained silence.

"When will I see you again?" I felt my face flush and tried to fight back the desperation in my voice. It was like a scene in a cheesy old Elvis movie: the departing soldier and his doleful, clinging girlfriend. By the time Blair returned in late August, I would have wrapped up my summer job in Toronto and be heading back to Massachusetts to finish my degree. I noticed his fresh army haircut, the line of exposed white skin along his neck and around his ears, but I was too wrapped up in myself to sense his pre-boot-camp jitters.

"I don't know when I'll be back. I'm not in charge of the arrangements." Of course: the army, with its red tape and bafflegab, was always calling the shots in our relationship.

In front of my rooming house, Blair pulled away from me. "I've got to go . . . I'll write."

I didn't want to hear that. I wanted him to say that even though he was going off to Gagetown, he had chosen me over the army.

• • •

That summer, I walked to my job through campus and down University Avenue, past the landmarks of our romance. At night, I sat in my dingy room with the windows wide open, trying to catch the non-existent breeze. I scoured the two letters that arrived from Gagetown for hidden meaning, but found only cheerful reports about machine guns and tank fire. So much for being enlightened and self-reliant. I was pathetic, somebody's girlfriend staring at a phone that never rang.

I wanted to, but I knew I couldn't blame the army for all of my misery. In the eight months Blair and I had known each other, we had changed positions as if we were dancing the Dashing White Sergeant. Now, he was the one who wanted to slow down, and I was in a hurry.

How had love melted my resistance to our relationship but not his? I lay on my bed and tried to shut out the whine of cicadas. I remembered the regimental motto on one of Blair's T-shirts: *Dileas Gu Brath*. Faithful Forever. Where did I fit into that phrase? What chance did I stand?

At the end of the summer, we had each survived our separate boot camps. The army delivered Blair from Gagetown and released me from my stew of sour desolation. Just the two of us at last, we held onto each other, took a breath and jumped into the future.

• • •

The love triangle went more smoothly when we lived in different cities. Blair stayed on in Toronto to go to law school, and I started graduate school in Ottawa—close enough for occasional weekend visits, but far enough away from the minutiae of his military life. As we approached the end of our studies, we wrestled with the idea of getting married and moving back to Calgary. We'd been away the better part of a decade. Could we go back? If we stayed in southern Ontario, within reach of the regiment, could we stay together? I wasn't sure how we would manage. Calgary promised not only good jobs and big sky, but for me, the end of Blair's military career. Blair still didn't see the military situation the way I did. He mused about joining the Calgary Highlanders, a sister organization to his Toronto regiment. He was close to qualifying as a captain; he'd spent summers with the Canadian Forces on bases in New Brunswick and Ontario, and one in Yellowknife, but hadn't had the chance at what reservists considered the big prize in the mid-1980s: a posting overseas at one of the NATO bases in Germany. Blair found an articling job at a law firm in Calgary; as for his military future, we were still miles apart.

Blair arrived in Calgary several months after me. A few days before our wedding, he stepped out of his car on my parents' driveway. The moustache was gone. I ran my fingers along his smooth upper lip. "Is this a sign?"

He whispered in my ear. "It was just a moustache."

The day before the wedding, a telegram arrived from the lieutenant colonel of the 48th Highlanders, welcoming me to the regimental family. *Dileus gu brath*, he'd signed off. Faithful forever. The words were a jab, a provocation. I fought the urge to crumple the page, and with it the army's presumptuous claim on what they thought belonged to them. I was a fool to think geography would stand in the way of the infantry and its objective.

Blair's new colleagues at the law firm knew little about the militia and offered him no encouragement to resume his military career. Though I complained from time to time about Blair's workload, I knew the drive to move up the legal ranks from associate to partner was my ally when it came to Blair's decision about the militia. Where would he find the time? When I was expecting our first child, I found it harder not to badger Blair for a final decision. Now it wasn't just about me. In the last weeks of my pregnancy, I'd feel spasms of fear along with the Braxton Hicks contractions. I didn't want my grandmother's life in the forties. For most of a decade when her children were small, her marriage consisted of an absentee soldier husband who saw his family on furlough. I didn't want to raise our children on my own, and I knew I didn't have to. It seemed obvious to me: we had the good luck to live in peaceful times in a peaceful country where individuals could choose whether or not they wanted to devote part of their lives to military service. The militia was for young, single people, not those with families and full and demanding civilian lives.

I should remember when and where Blair told me he'd decided his military career was over, the same way I can recall the detailed landscape of our courtship. Were we driving? Doing the dishes? All I remember is the sensation of release, as if the battle I'd been waging for years had finally come to an end.

• • •

Blair's regimental kilt, dress jacket and sporran hang in a garment bag in the bedroom closet. When he wears highland attire to a black-tie event, his bare knees and the *skean dhu* tucked in the band of his wool socks always cause a stir. Now that the military is a historical footnote in our lives, I've come to enjoy the way Blair's outfit takes the attention off me. The kilt can stay upstairs, but I've relegated the rest of Blair's army memorabilia to the basement. Army-issue green towels in the rag bag, an old helmet cover and a canvas satchel in the children's dress-up trunk, ammo boxes filled with shoe polish in the pantry. That day the basement flooded, the water services guy also spotted an 8-by-10 framed snapshot of two soldiers on our workshop wall. The photo hadn't always hung there. Blair valued the gift from one of his army friends, but I did not. Early on in our marriage, I'd moved the photo from display in the family room to a box in the basement. I ignored Blair's grumbling; I didn't need to be reminded of his buddy and the way he'd made me feel like I was an interloper in his military friendship with Blair. A few years ago, I softened and found a place for the snapshot above the paint cans in the workshop. Surely after all these years, I told myself, I could take a few steps on the high road. When I told Blair about my magnanimous gesture, he laughed. He still thinks my view of things military is simplistic. These days, our discussions about war aren't much different from those we had when we were courting: me with the luxury of a bird's-eye view, and Blair viewing conflict more closely with a sense of the trenches.

I study the photograph now. Two soldiers stand on a sand dune. Helmets camouflaged with dried grass, faces obscured by dark scarves, rifles at the ready. Blair's friend has scrawled on the bottom left corner: To Blair, my "brother in arms." I have to look closely to tell which one is my husband. I can't see his expression, but I know he's grinning under that bandana and his eyes are bright—the battle fatigues, the weapons, the belly-crawling over sand dunes, the hiding from the pretend enemy. It's taken me 30 years, but I think I get it. When Blair joined the army, he opened himself up to the unknown. He took risks. He wanted to be part of something bigger than himself. Not so different than falling in love.

COMING HOME TO A NEW WORLD

Ryan Flavelle

Drunk. And I mean, too drunk. I am sitting at the swim-up bar of the Azia Resort in Cyprus, and I've been drinking beer, shots, highballs and whatever else seemed like a good idea for the last five hours. The whole world is my friend. I am young, strong, fit and excited. I have survived the last seven months in Afghanistan, and I am on my way home. I am on "decompression," a three-day vacation in Cyprus that allows us a chance to party together before we get back to Canada. The army isn't stupid. It realizes that its soldiers should have a chance to debauch themselves before they arrive home and are released amongst the Canadian population. I am doing my best to debauch myself. Indeed, Bacchus—the Roman god of madness, mirth and wine—is very much in evidence as the 80 or so soldiers inhabiting the resort drink and smoke and laugh. They fight each other, laugh together and—by the end of the night—cry together. The tour is rehashed, and the stories that we lived through are retold. For the moment, the dark points are forgotten, although they will eventually make their appearance.

. . .

Five days before we arrived in Cyprus, I was sitting in the back of a Light Armoured Vehicle (LAV), chewing tobacco and smoking at the same time, breathing dust. I tasted the too-familiar grit of the moon dust, and inhaled acrid tobacco that made me feel a little sick to my stomach. I felt the smoothness of my tan combat gloves, which still had partially dried raisins stuck to them.

These raisins had gotten stuck to my gloves when I leaned back into a pile of them a month earlier. We had blown the metal door of a mud-walled compound with C4 explosive and searched the compound for Improvised Explosive Devices (IEDs). But when we "cleared in," we were confronted only with freshly dried grapes, arrayed chronologically along the floor: dried raisins closest to the door and recently harvested grapes near the far wall of the 10-metre enclosed space. We didn't find any IEDs—only raisins, homemade wine and an ideal defensive position. We were in Pashmul, north of the Arghandab River and south of Patrol Base Wilson. We were in Taliban territory.

After two mostly sleepless nights, we were back at our base, Sperwan Ghar—a mountain of dust bristling with antennae. That was my last dismounted operation, and after a month of radio shifts and a handover to the Royal Canadian Regiment, I was on the road home—back to Kandahar Airfield (KAF) and, if all went according to plan, Calgary by way of Cyprus. The raisin jelly stuck to my otherwise smooth gloves was the only tangible reminder I had left of that compound.

Earlier, a man I knew and respected had died on these same roads, on his way back to KAF and home. I had heard the incident play out on the radio and watched it scroll slowly across a computer screen.

A LAV had rolled after an IED blew up underneath it. Seven people were injured and one killed, all on their last trip before home. So I was understandably nervous during this final LAV ride of my seven-month stay in the country of Afghanistan. But there was absolutely no point in worrying. Something would either happen or it wouldn't; there was nothing I could do to change it. The freedom to choose whether or not to take part in things that directly affected my safety had all but been removed. I had no choice but to accept whatever came as the will of fate, God or physics—depending on the day. *Insha'Allah*.

We made it back to KAF—that bizarre world of red flags, floppy hats, Tim Hortons and the never-ending smell of human waste—and we were reintegrated into the regular rules and norms of the military system once again. We played *Battlefield 2*. KAF housed a double-wide ATCO-style trailer filled with two rows of computers that had almost every popular video game loaded onto them. While we waited to go home, the trailer filled up and we shot computerized versions of ourselves for hours. The game was broken into teams: terrorists vs. Americans. I found that virtual reality was infinitely more comfortable and fun than reality had been.

• • •

It is 36 hours later, and I'm drinking beers in the Azia Resort swimming pool. Nothing in the world is wrong. I haven't seen alcohol in almost three months, since my European break from the war with my girlfriend. It is affecting me more quickly than normal. I am drinking with the company headquarters section—the group I had been attached to since I started pre-training forever ago in Shilo, Manitoba. These were the guys who had sat with me in the grape huts of Panjway—and together, we have worked our way down the street to a beach bar. British waitresses, who tell us that they are in Cyprus on working vacations, are no doubt utterly tired of being hit on by Canadians. But they are tanned and young, and we are tanned and young, and flush with cash. More than one person at the table proposes marriage, and other—less honourable—relations to them. The night progresses and my head begins to bob. The conversations take place further and further away, and the world becomes more fragmentary, my interactions with it less controlled. I am "right shittered," as those in the army would call it. I lurch through faltering steps back to my room—much earlier than I had planned—and fall face first onto my mattress. In the split second before I am fast asleep, I am conscious of a happiness I haven't known for seven months, or indeed for my entire life. I have made it through a war, and I am going home.

I dream of a perfect Canadian autumn, the leaves changing in the provincial park by my house, and the sun in my girlfriend's hair, bringing out the highlights as she looks back at me with blue eyes and a coy smile. I dream, as I so often did while overseas, of being reunited with my friends, telling stories and playing video games like we had in university. Back then I thought that I knew everything there was to know about the world. But now, I dream of the world that I remember leaving, without realizing that it no longer exists. I have changed, and so has my home. I know less, although I have experienced more. I have seen things that made me realize that I knew very little about the world. Things that I wished I hadn't seen: starving children, mangled bodies and limbs torn to shreds, the eyes of evil men from across an opium field.

• • •

Drunk—again, and again, too drunk. It is three weeks since I got home from Afghanistan, and two months since I finished my last dismounted cordon-and-search operation in Pashmul. I am in Calgary at the Colonel Pryde dinner, named after a former commanding officer who had served in the Second World War. I'm still technically on leave, but I wouldn't miss Colonel Pryde for the world. It is my unit's annual social event, known as a "mess dinner." It is planned by the youngest officer in the unit and any new guys who don't know better than to volunteer to help out. We are in for a lavish affair complete with polished silver candelabras, four courses, a band and loyal toasts with port. Husbands, wives, girlfriends, boyfriends and friends are invited. It is a chance to "break bread" as a unit family. It is also a chance to drink beer with one's military friends. I love Colonel Pryde. I spend the night before the dinner watching *Forrest Gump, Platoon* and *Black Hawk Down* while polishing my boots to a mirror shine. I agonize over the placement of each pin on my newly dry-cleaned uniform. Finally I put it on and feel resplendent in the badges and buttons that the Canadian government has issued me. For the first time, I have a medal on my chest: the General Campaign Star (GCS) with ISAF bar (which means that I was under the command of the International Security Assistance Force while overseas). I think it looks good, if a little lonely. A lot of effort went into earning this medal. I had the fortune or misfortune (depending on who and when you ask) of being in combat. My medal is supposed to represent those trials and tribulations.

After I make it to the dinner, I look around at those of my friends who have more medals than me but have not experienced combat. I am consumed with green envy, the worst of human emotions. I drink most of the expensive wine that I bought to share with my friends. I have two beers on the go by the time that we stand with our hands on our chairs, awaiting the entrance of the head table. By the time the appetizer is served, I am sullen, upset at my close friend who earned a commander's commendation while overseas. The joy and optimism that accompanied my walking into the dinner has been replaced by jealousy and anger. My words become slurred. A new corporal vomits red wine into the tablecloth; perhaps this affair won't be as high-class as I'd envisioned. By the time that the toasts are being made, I am belligerent—as I had learned to be while working with the infantry in Afghanistan. Instead of my friends and fellow soldiers, some of whom I've known for years, I see nothing but WOGs (the infantry expression for those who do not fight. I don't even know what it stands for—Waste of Groceries? WithOut Guns?). When the speaker begins to discuss the freedom of the press, and its importance as an institution within Canadian democracy, I heckle him. He isn't talking about what is important to me: soldiers, combat, the military. I want to be released from this room, which has become claustrophobic. I want to be outside, smoking and railing against the world.

It feels like this is no longer my world, my military home, my family. I say a few harsh words that I later regret. I ask my friend what he has done to earn his rack of medals, because I feel self-conscious that I only have one. I ask it confrontationally, as if I am better than he is because I walked with the infantry in Afghanistan, even though he walked with the infantry in Bosnia. But he forgives me; in fact, I don't think he ever really held it against me. When I bring up the conversation later, with a sheepdog expression, he passes it off as nothing, merely the drunken ramblings of someone who deserved to be drunk. Apparently the tour had allotted me a certain amount of absolution.

About a month after I get home, I go for a walk with my girlfriend in the waning yellow autumn light. We hold hands and meander through residential Calgary, and the sun picks up the highlights in her hair, which I had long imagined in the darkest days of my war. As we walk, we hear someone re-roofing their house, the nail gun audible but unseen. "Crack, crack, crack . . . Crack, crack, crack," it goes off steadily, as machine guns do. I am back on an endless march through the grape fields of Panjway, feeling the hair on my neck stand up, wanting to run away or take cover. I keep walking in a cold sweat, and my girlfriend squeezes my hand.

Later, when I go out for lunch with some friends, I am cognizant of an incoherent and all-encompassing rage that is spawned of nothing, and continues for no reason. My hands shake and ball into fists; I stay silent as the conversation takes place without me. Finally I get up, drop a 20-dollar bill with a scowl, and leave. Once more I feel enclosed and need to be outside, alone. Home doesn't feel right.

I go to a movie with my parents and sit in the back of their car, as I did when I was a child. We get stuck at a red light that, my father feels, was poorly designed, as it does not allow a sufficient number of cars to enter the mall parking lot. This is Calgary, supposedly the road-rage capital of Canada. It seems so stupid and petty that these are the problems of our society: that people passionately care about making the light. Problems like this had simply ceased to exist for me when I was overseas. There were so many truly important things happening around us, even on a quiet day. We didn't care about lights; we cared about IEDs. But that world had ceased to exist when I got off the plane, and—although it was hard for me to admit—I missed it. I felt like I was wasting time, walking the treadmill of North American life without a purpose. My time in Afghanistan had felt chock full of purpose.

As the year progresses and I tell stumbling stories to my military friends, desperately attempting to contextualize my experiences, I also learn about their tours—the good, the bad and the ugly. As I reintegrate into Canadian society, I also reintegrate into reservist society, and I begin to realize that only fate separated me and my experiences from them and theirs. "There, but for the grace of God, go I." *Insha'Allah*.

● ● ●

It is 10 months since I got home from Afghanistan and I am nursing a beer. It is a brilliant late summer day and I am wearing my best suit and a pink tie. I am in rural Alberta, 10 kilometres outside Rocky Mountain House, near my in-laws' acreage. I have just been married, and I am at the Bingly Hall, a stubby Quonset hut with a baseball diamond outside of it. There are pillows nailed to the roof (although I'm not sure why), and my family and I had spent the previous day decorating it. My wife is glowing in her dress, and I am conscious that I am starting something worthwhile. The twilight lengthens, but the night is warm. I reconnect with friends and family and feel joy in their company. I feel good and right, and at peace. I married the girl with the bluest eyes, who loves me and asks only that I love her in return.

She had spent the long vigil of my tour wondering why everyone was so worried about her. She felt that I was doing what I wanted to do, and we should all be so lucky. While I was overseas, she emailed me almost every day. She sent packages, books, letters and pictures. She worked hard on maintaining the strength and durability of our relationship throughout the seven months that I was in Afghanistan, and she became the foundation of my post-war life. She is someone I could always turn to, in spite of nail guns and incoherent rage.

At first I didn't know how to act when I was around her again; I didn't know how much of my life I should let her into. I felt that she didn't want to know about the things I'd experienced, or, worse, that she didn't deserve to know about them. But slowly, the companionship and sparks of passion returned. We regained each other's trust. We watched every episode of *The Office* together, compliments of a store on the boardwalk in KAF that I had stopped at on the way home. It was good to begin to laugh again, and hold hands again, and we were once again friends, and in love. She encouraged me to tell my story, and she listened while I told it. She edited every word of my book and made me feel like it was worth doing. She gave me a safe place to work through my memories.

I still think about the tour every single day, but the memories no longer have the same power or sting to them. I have finished the transition back to civilian life. The roles and identities that had made me who I was before the war were familiar and readily accessible. Even though the perfect home I had imagined while in Afghanistan was obscured by the rage that had accompanied my return, I found myself busily constructing a more permanent foundation. I went to grad school to study the Canadian military, strategy and the First World War. I was once more consumed by books and theories about the conduct of military operations. But this study was so different than the visceral power of bloody war that I began to think that the two bear almost no relationship to one another.

War has the power to fundamentally change who people are and how they act. Everyone I know who has experienced the dust and danger of Afghanistan came back changed. Usually this change is subtle, but we have seen a different world—one that challenged our beliefs about humanity and ourselves. When I came home, I found it difficult to reintegrate into a society that has not experienced these things. I forgot how to be a civilian when I was in Afghanistan, and it has taken significant time and practice to relearn that skill. Now I can go back to screaming at red lights for making me late, but I also know that it really doesn't matter.

Things will happen if they happen. *Insha'Allah.*

SNAPSHOTS: LIFE, PEACE AND COFFEE ON THE HOME FRONT

Ellen Kelly

1. Spring 2011. Battalion Park, Calgary, beside the Westhills shopping complex. Focus on four white-washed fieldstone numbers embedded in the hillside.

I can see three of the numerals, 51, 137 and 151, clearly as I leave Starbucks with my grande half-sweet hazelnut latte; the fourth, 113, is harder to spot, higher on the hillside and in a flatter area. Each digit is approximately 36 metres high. Most people, I have discovered, regard them as simply part of the landscape, but I know how they got there—and more importantly, I know what they mean. They represent my right to enjoy an overpriced coffee in a mega shopping area where I am free to wander and shop as I please. They represent hard work done long ago, and now, remembrance. They pay tribute to members of the Canadian Expeditionary Forces sent to fight during the First World War.

I've always felt a personal attachment to these numbers for two reasons. I am the daughter of a First World War veteran and have a responsibility to my father not to let the significance of the numbers be forgotten. My father was an infantry soldier and member of the 137th Battalion who helped lug those rocks up the hill in 1916 and who later saw action in France and Belgium. There aren't many of us direct descendents left. My father was 59 years old when I was born, a late-in-life baby to a man whose marriage to my mother also came late in his life. I do the math and marvel that if Dad was alive today, in 2011, he'd be 123 years old.

My father didn't talk about the war that marked him deeply before his life as a family man began. Old enough to be my grandfather, he was the embodiment of Presbyterian fortitude and stony acceptance. He was raised in Scotland in the late 1800s, when religious training and education were handled by the same severe institution. The trenches, mustard gas, fear, disease and death were memories best left unshared. He would answer direct questions as briefly as possible, if at all. "Did you get shot?" "No." Did you see people get killed?" "Yes." "Did you ever shoot anyone, Daddy?" No answer. "What was it like over there?" He would rub his lower legs, damaged during his time in France, where he stood in trenches full of water, blood and human waste for days on end. Then he would walk to the window and stare into the distance, often for a very long time. He was not a talkative person and likely was often driven to silence by his small, curious daughter.

"Daddy, tell me about the war. What did you do there?"

"Och, nothing that would interest you. Don't ask so many questions."

I would persist and he would walk away, often to the refuge of his vegetable garden. He loved growing things but hated picked flowers, said they reminded him that all things die.

2. Post-1918, Calgary, Alberta. A black-and-white snapshot of Amelia Stephen and her three children shows the family outside their home. Amelia draws her small family close as they squint into the camera. Focus on the space behind Amelia, where husband and father John Stephen should have been standing.

After the war, my father worked at several jobs, some in Calgary and some in the municipal districts surrounding the growing city. During this time, he was also helping to raise his brother's family. The brothers had signed up together, but only one returned; brother John was killed at Vimy in May 1917, leaving a wife and three children behind. The children were small and widows' compensation was negligible, so my father's duty was to become the family's surrogate father. He met my mother, a high school friend of the older of his nieces, when he needed an experienced horsewoman to ride a jumping horse he had purchased. The niece recommended her friend, my mother, a farm girl who rode horses all the time. Fame and fortune didn't follow the adventure into the horse ring, but romance did. My father met and married my mother, 25 years his junior, in 1932. I imagine that conflicting feelings and judgements from my mother's mother and brother when she married a man old enough to be her father, and jealousy from my father's surrogate family, are what drove discussion of this time from both my parents underground.

3. June 2011. Peacekeeper Park, Calgary. A Wall of Honour constructed in 2004 and projected to last 60 years has already been filled, so a second wall has been added to include all Canadian Forces members who have lost their lives during peacekeeping missions and in Afghanistan. Focus on the name peacekeeper. *Focus on the statue of a soldier presenting a doll to a child.*

The second reason I feel an attachment to the Signal Hill numbers has to do with Canada's involvement in Afghanistan and the unsettling fact that I know young men who have enlisted with the goal of being deployed. Being fortunate enough to live in a country that has been at peace for almost my entire lifetime, I wonder if this is madness or human nature. I imagine my father's reasoning was a call to duty to defend "his King and Country," but his deployment also offered him two trips to Scotland to visit his parents and siblings. These were the only times he returned "home" and would not have been possible had he not been stationed in England during some of his time overseas.

A soldier fighting in the First World War prayed he would be one of the relatively few survivors; young men soldier today hoping they won't be one of the relatively small number of casualties. However, although almost 100 years later, young men and women might be less bound to "King and Country," the varied reasons for enlisting might be similar. Adventure. A compulsion to fight? A competitive need to win? Or perhaps a deep commitment to what the deployment represents? A desire to make changes in the world? Will the names of the young men I met while working in the guidance department of a local high school be engraved on the recently constructed Wall of Honour in Peacekeeper Park or, as older, wiser returning soldiers, will they take their families to this memorial wall, touch the engraved names of their lost comrades and remember, just as my father remembered when he visited the stone numerals on the hill? I sense a connection that spans a century.

4. Summer 1953. Signal Hill. The view is from a gravel road, which in the future will become Richmond Road. In the foreground: windswept prairie. To the southeast, leased land recently returned to the Sarcee Tsuu T'ina Nation and to the west, the Rocky Mountains. Focus on the hillside to the north.

Daddy is driving. A basket with our lunch sits between him and Mom on the front seat of the late-thirties model Chevy sedan. I am five years old and we are going on a picnic adventure. We bump along on gravel roads and the car fills with dust; it makes me sneeze and I am hot, thirsty, cranky.

Finally we are there. We get out of the car in a field of tall grass and thistle. Daddy picks me up, looks south, to where he spent almost a year in Sarcee Camp, "learning to be a soldier," he tells me. Then he looks northwest to the hillside, points at rocks that look to me like rubble.

Daddy pushes back his tweed cap and traces numbers in the air with his finger. Mom, dressed in her best housedress, holds his arm as the tall grass brushes her bare legs. With her other hand, she shades her eyes from the sun and wind, and nods. They lean into each other and gaze at the hillside. He knows exactly where the numbers lay; she pulls her cardigan around her shoulders and takes in the expanse of hill, rocks and brush. I am busy with childish interests— chasing grasshoppers, plucking wildflowers, picking the burrs out of my socks.

Mom winds new film into the Kodak box camera, follows Daddy's finger and takes a picture of the hillside. I eat my sandwich and swat mosquitoes, trying not to think of the long, dusty ride home.

• • •

In April 1915 work began to create Sarcee Camp on leased land that was part of what was then called the Sarcee Indian Reserve. By summer 1916 the camp, consisting mainly of thousands of white bell tents in neat rows, housed 12 infantry battalions and some specialized units—almost 15,000 men. Battalions were deployed and others took their place. Eventually, 45,000 soldiers from across Alberta passed through the camp. Pictures taken between 1915 and 1918 remind me, with my limited understanding, of a giant Boy Scout jamboree.

How many mugs of gut-rot coffee were prepared over campfires and on cookstoves and drunk black or diluted with canned milk during the years soldiers were trained at the camp? Surely, these soldiers thought about their futures while drinking coffee from army-issue tin cups just as I contemplate my father's past as I enjoy my specialty coffee on this same site.

Many battalions left their numbers on the hillside, but today only four remain; the rest have been absorbed into the land by time and nature. The 113th Lethbridge Highlands Infantry Battalion, the 51st Canadian Infantry Battalion from Edmonton, the 151st Central Alberta Battalion (Red Deer), and "Calgary's Own" 137th Battalion were "recruitment battalions," whose members were sent to supplement other units as more soldiers were needed. Many remained loyal to their original battalions. When the men of the 137th returned from the war, they saw the numbers not as a training exercise or as a way to combat boredom, but as my father did—as a remembrance of those who died on the battlefields. However, for many years the rock memorials were disregarded and they almost completely disappeared, buried by blowing soil and overgrown by prairie grass.

5. 1916. Sarcee Camp. The photograph is of my handsome, smiling, young father in First World War dress uniform: forage cap at a cocky slant, khaki tunic and pants, puttees. Focus on the look of anticipation and pride on my father's face.

Streetcar service ran from Calgary to the camp gates for the convenience of soldiers and their visiting families, the kind of transit service the City of Calgary struggles with today as it builds the southwest route of the modern LRT system. Soldiers returning to camp at night must have marvelled at the glow from newly born flares in the distant southwest sky. The oilfield at Turner Valley began producing in 1914, and the sky blushed with the promise of a province's future, less brutal than the imminent fires in Europe that the soldiers would soon face. A bustling community known as Sarcee City flourished just outside the camp; it included a thriving commercial area where a soldier with wages earned during his time at the camp (which, in some cases, was almost a year) could buy anything his heart and body desired. I can only imagine that my father, young and single, might have enjoyed his time spent here but was probably influenced by the presence of his more settled brother, whose wife and children likely visited often.

At Sarcee Camp, whitewashed fieldstones outlined roads, walkways and unit perimeters. Soldiers also constructed their unit badges from these rocks, displaying them at the entrance to their assigned areas in the tent city. Scattered whitewashed stones can still be found in the southern area of where the camp once stood.

Exactly why men carried rocks two kilometres uphill and reconstructed their battalion numbers on what was then called Cairn Hill is not clear. Perhaps it was the next logical step in a place where there was a need for training exercises, a large hill and an abundance of rocks.

The exercise may have been a disciplinary strategy or a make-work project to defer the boredom of waiting.

Twenty of these markers remained in 1924, but gradually the earth reclaimed the stones. By the 1950s, when my father was in his sixties and I was five or six, only a sharp eye and a good memory could point out the numbers.

6. Mid-1960s. Calgary. East of 4th Street lies Central Memorial Park and the Cenotaph, a location for ceremonies remembering Canadian Forces Members killed in the First and Second World Wars. To the west is the Colonel Belcher (Veterans') Hospital, a refuge for damaged survivors, Canadian veterans wounded in military actions. Focus on the relatively new hospital wing. The 250-bed Colonel Belcher Hospital was opened in December 1943, with the words, "May this fine hospital be a lasting memory to those whose courage, sacrifice and devotion enable us to remain in freedom. Here may we be privileged to give a helping hand, a kindly word and guiding inspiration to those young heroes who shall, in the inevitable destiny of battle, have to sojourn here awhile." Those were foreboding words for many returning soldiers who would spend the rest of their lives in the facility and for their families, who were governed by strict visiting regulations, or relatives who could not face the suffering enclosed in those walls and spent lifetimes in guilt, apart from their loved ones, never visiting.

Patients had been moved from the original Colonel Belcher Hospital site (est. 1919) on 8th Avenue and 5th Street SW. Shortly after the 1943 opening, the federal government increased support for military hospitals across the country, and by May 1944 an expansion was already underway. In 1952, land west of the Belcher was purchased for the construction of a four-storey addition. The new wing was opened in November 1956, and services were in place just as many vets of that era, including my father, were beginning to need them.

My father's health issues—after a heart attack in the mid-1950s and resulting progressive congestive heart failure as well as his advancing years—made hospital visits to regulate medications and treat associated conditions an ongoing and increasingly regular occurrence. My mother, who realized that she needed to become a family income provider after years of mothering, took a 10-month nurse's aide course and graduated as valedictorian of her class. She was excellent at her job, but as she told us years later, her main purpose was to be able to take proper care of my father as his health deteriorated.

Regulations didn't permit children to visit hospital patients, but by the time I was 14 and in high school, I was allowed. Never having been inside a hospital before, I looked upon it as an adventure. Mom was uncertain: I had been protected from "distasteful" matters, things "not for children's eyes and ears." She worried about the impact visiting would have on me, and rightfully so. Initially I was intrigued, and I spent some time determined to become a nurse. However, by the time I graduated from high school, I was overwhelmed by the sights, sounds, smells and hopelessness of the hospital and patients, and much to my parents' disappointment, decided not to pursue a career in health care.

Dad's hospital stays, which lasted from two or three days to a couple of weeks and occurred three or four times a year, blend into each other in my memories—the walk from my high school to the hospital, a couple of games of cribbage, Dad propped up in bed or sitting on the edge, me sitting cross-legged on the bed, then a kiss on the cheek and the bus ride home. In the background of these visits, nurses quietly worked in starched white aprons and stiff white caps. The peaceful, dusk-like ambiance and calming green walls come to mind. And everything was clean. Always, the housekeeping staff were dusting, mopping, changing beds and fluffing pillows.

But in the foreground were the sights and sounds that I was able to ignore at the time but that remain as vivid now as they were then. Dad's room was most often on the third floor of the wing that ran along 12th Avenue. Outside the door at the south end of that wing (in summer), inside the door (in winter) and beside the elevator gathered a rag-tag welcoming committee. Veterans of the Second World War or Korea, some old like my father and some younger, smoked and gossiped with each other. There were always six or eight, many attached to intravenous stands and most missing something—an arm, a leg, the ability to see or hear or hold themselves erect. I had been told by my mother not to talk to these men. Some made rude, suggestive remarks or winked, called me sweetheart and baby, and reached out to touch me. They didn't scare me, but they did make me feel uncomfortable and I hurried by quickly, thankful that I could move faster than them. Others said, "Hello, how are you, nice to see you" in a most respectful way, and I regret snubbing them indiscriminately on my race to and from the safety of my father's room. I often wonder what happened to the old veteran who searched under beds for snakes until he was led, crying, back to his room, or to the young man who wandered the halls asking visitors, "Do you know me? Do you know who I am?"

Mostly, my dad's ward was quiet. But each visit was punctuated at intervals by distant screams, shouts and the repetitive, anguished pleading from residents in a ward farther down the hall. But while these men wept and wailed, it seemed to have nothing to do with my father.

How naive I was! I wish now that I had understood more, wanted to know more, but the hospital had an air of shame about it, housing all those maimed and damaged men. At the time it seemed better to leave it alone. After all, my father was never there for long. I much preferred to play crib with him at home in our living room.

Nonetheless I visited, not wanting to disappoint Dad or face the wrath of my mother, who found my teenage years very difficult. I realize now that she was stressed beyond my comprehension, but her tension and my need to grow often led to angry outbursts. She expected obedience, but I was a teenager and moving into the world of dating, friends with cars and a need to challenge. Mom was often at her wits' end, saying, "If you behave like that it'll kill your father, you know." I never truly believed it, yet it kept me in line for several years.

Dad and I are playing cribbage in his room at the Colonel Belcher Hospital during one of his many admissions during the last decade of his life. I am a teenager, a flower child, and I believe in peace and love and freedom. I do not understand the price of peace and love and freedom. I don't believe in wars and soldiering, especially as I listen to the wailing men on other wards who, my father tells me, suffer from shell shock and who, in their minds, have never returned from the battlefields of the First or Second World War or Korea. I mention glibly that the First World War was supposed to be the war to end all wars, and Dad sighs and says, "Aye, love, it was."

As a teenager and young adult, I didn't associate the young men who were being injured and killed in Vietnam with the patients at the hospital. I felt contempt for the American war but never for my father and his compatriots. For me, there was a huge disconnect between young soldiers and the veterans. It may have been a trick of the mind but it took me years to figure out that one led to the other.

7. June 2011. Battalion Park, self-directed walking tour. In the far distance, the Rockies; nearby are new subdivisions. A series of plaques explaining Battalion Park, Camp Sarcee and Canada's participation in the First World War are distributed along the wooden path and staircases. Focus on the shopping complex below, where Starbucks is visible among the many shops.

Dad sometimes talked about Sarcee Camp and good times there— soccer games and picnics, visits from family, a "grand idea" to walk to the mountains that seemed so much closer than they actually were. But his overseas memories were locked behind piercing blue eyes that searched out the stone markers on the side of a grass- and brush-covered hill. He knew exactly where the stone numerals were and because it was important to him, I told him I could see them too, although the picture in Dad's mind seemed far clearer than the debris on the hillside.

By 1967, Dad was in poor health and not part of the advocacy group determined to save the numerals, but I'm certain he was both thrilled at the idea of having the memorial restored and hurt by the indifference of the government. He passed away in 1972 without knowing that the landmark would be restored with a park built on the site.

As I drink my latte, I look up at the whitewashed numerals on the hillside and recall the stories I've read about the horrors soldiers faced in the Great War and the memories of the families they left behind. It gives me an inkling of what was locked away in my father's head. I think of the young men I know now and contemplate how much may have changed, yet how much has stayed the same. And I wonder what the numbers on the hillside, the memorial to my father's war to end all wars, really signify? My ability to buy a specialty coffee, to shop where I please and to expect an affluent lifestyle comes at a dubious cost, and I am overwhelmingly grateful that I have the right to question it.

THE RESERVIST

Barb Howard

Once a year I attend a parade. The occasion is a combined celebration of St. George's Day and the birthday of the King's Own Calgary Regiment. The event consists of a parade to a church, a church service (also an annual appearance for me) and a reception at Mewata Armoury. At the reception I am sometimes asked to present the Howard Trophy, which is a miniature tank resting on a small wooden platform. I never know how this presentation should be executed, whose hand to shake (the trophy is given to a troop) or when to sit back down. The entire affair is so completely out of the realm of my day-to-day life that it is like visiting another planet. Planet Military. That's where my dad, Major General William A. Howard, CM, CMM, CD, QC, used to live.

Since my dad was an army reservist, I had more exposure to Planet Military than most Canadians in my age group. But that exposure was many steps removed from the real thing, that is, from "the profession of arms." For instance, army-speak became a casual part of our family lexicon. Within our family of six, anyone younger, and therefore of a lower rank, was referred to as 2IC, second in command. A teenager whose whereabouts were unknown on a Friday night was AWOL or MIA. A hangover was a SIW, a self-inflicted wound.

The abbreviations were fun—like talking pig Latin, except sometimes harder to translate. A woman at the airport once asked my dad, "Is your first name really Emgen?" because she had seen his luggage tag that said "MGen Howard." Our wonder at how anyone could be so ignorant helped the Emgen anecdote grow into family folklore and was evidence of how, like all codes, the army-speak insulated us, bound us together. But we didn't really think about what army-speak meant. Correction—I didn't think about it. My parents both served in the Second World War and knew the circumstances and issues that might prompt a real SIW, the emotional and practical consequences that ensued from a real MIA listing. As for me, I suspect I just felt abundantly clever when I flavoured my speech with the occasional military term, or entertained my friends with a wacky army-esque anecdote about my dad, or generally spouted off to show I knew some stuff, or had access to some stuff, that my friends didn't.

• • •

But my siblings and I were not cadets. We were familiar with a few of the trappings, but plain and simple, we did not "get" the army. The regimentation. The shouting. The marching. The uniforms. Making our beds. None of it worked on any level for us. It wasn't just the system. I thought the cadets themselves were weird. And I know I wasn't alone in that superficial judgement, especially in the 1970s. There's nothing like insanely short hair, whitewall ears and rifle-straight posture to make a kid stand out, in a bad way, in junior high school. Paying attention in Canadian history class—as did the lone cadet in my junior high—didn't help either. Who paid attention to *that*?

I viewed my dad as a grown-up extension of weird cadets (especially since he was a vocal and enthusiastic supporter of the Army Cadet League of Canada) and as the epitome of geekdom. The officer and reservist aspect of his military involvement made everything worse. It seemed to me, in those days, that he was a pretend soldier. Dinner meetings in Ottawa rather than trench digging on a war-torn distant continent. Snifters of brandy warmed over a crystal candle-set rather than freeze-dried field rations eaten under a flurry of artillery flak. My dad wasn't going to be in combat. I doubt he held a weapon after basic training circa 1939. (On the other hand, there is a slew of casualties, myself included, willing to testify that he was a master at going verbally *mano a mano*.)

Despite their active role with the Canadian Forces in Afghanistan, I've heard that reservists are still occasionally referred to within the army as SAS (Saturday and summer) soldiers or Toons, as in cartoons. Only seen on weekends. And indeed, there was a cartoon quality to my dad. He was bald, fat and temperamental—all of which thankfully fit into the acceptable dad template in our fresh suburban neighbourhood. There were other dads almost as bald and fat and temperamental as my dad. The crucial difference was that none of them dressed up in uniforms and medals and went out to dinners, decorative swords hanging at their sides. None of them were escorted to and from the house in a staff car driven by a long-suffering soldier. An aide. Or, as my parents sometimes said, slipping to an earlier oh-so-British era (even though they weren't British), a "batman."

The aide didn't talk to kids. He sat in his car on our driveway, sometimes for hours, waiting for my dad to arrive home from work, change and get in the car for transportation to a military event. Or, if my dad was home, the aide stood, sweating, at the front door, attempting to ignore the jumpy dog spreading hair on his uniform, politely refusing my mother's entreaties to sit down in the living room. When my dad appeared the aide would deliver a sharp salute: four fingers to the brow, followed by a snap down. I would be looking at the aide and thinking, *Why is this young guy wasting his time doing this job?* And sure, he was probably thinking, *Why doesn't this spoiled little brat control her dog?*

The aide served two purposes, so far as I could tell. First, he prevented my dad from driving drunk. Drinking is time-honoured off-duty military recreation. My sister and I were repeatedly warned "watch out, girls—the highballs in the Officers' Mess are always doubles." The advice was lost on us. When/why would we ever, in our entire lives, be in the Officers' Mess? What cataclysmic event could occur that would find us surrounded by regimental memorabilia and green-suited men? Obviously, I did not foresee the Howard Trophy and the St. George's Day parade.

The second purpose of the aide seemed to be to perform sycophantic functions for my dad's benefit. There was no shortage of hop-to-ing, yes sir-ing, and general kowtowing to, and agreement with, whatever outlandish opinions my father proffered. In those days, all his opinions seemed outlandish to me. More money for the Armed Forces, more tanks, more programs for cadets.

Sometimes my dad eschewed the aide. For summer holidays, my dad drove us all to Vernon for the Army Cadet Camp. He kept the windows up, hermetically sealing the vehicle so as not to interfere with the air conditioning. He puffed on a House of Lords cigar for the entire six hours, while the air conditioning circulated a riptide of thick smoke throughout the car. Add in a full-throttle brass-and-drums eight-track version of the "Colonel Bogey March" and it should be clear why we never invited friends on vacation.

In Vernon, and at the tattoos and other cadet functions that we attended throughout the year as a family, there was usually a parade. The military loves a parade. And often a parade involves a row-by-row review of the troops by a high-ranking officer or dignitary. Thus, my most vivid memory of parades is of cadets fainting from the strain of remaining at attention for so long. Not just in the sweltering summer heat of Vernon, but in the sweltering heat at Currie Barracks and HMCS Tecumseh and Wainwright. "Oh that poor kid," my mother would say when a soldier slumped to the ground. "Why don't they tell them to squeeze their toes to keep the blood flowing?"

My parents never told me that one of the purposes of parades was to show the precise drill work of the sort that builds unit confidence and, historically, has helped win wars. They never said soldiers have to be tough and that a faint was, relative to the ultimate job soldiers train for, nothing. In fact, other than hauling us around to military activities and ensuring I knew a few superficial, mannerly details, my parents never tried to interest me in the Canadian Armed Forces at all. Perhaps, to use a favourite phrase of my dad's, they knew I "didn't have big enough balls for it." In any case, it was quite evident that my interest and attention in military matters was maxed out at the shallowest level. The result is that I know to pronounce khaki as "carky" and lieutenant as "lef-tenant" when I am around Canadian army people. As well, in the unlikely event that I am crisply marching with a large unit,

I know to "break step on a bridge" so as not to set the bridge into dangerous sway. But I had no idea what my dad, or the Canadian Forces, actually *did*. Perhaps that is partly a generational issue. I have many friends who, while knowing their parents' job titles or hobbies, never really knew exactly what their parents did. But the military, for my dad, was more than an interest. It intruded upon, and even shaped, most of our weekends (boiled hot dogs and food fights on Friday nights while mom and dad were out late "with army friends"), vacations (when I was five, we were marched—often literally—through England) and even Christmas morning (where we sat silently in front of the television, listening to the Queen's speech—our ersatz church service delivered by the commander-in-chief).

• • •

Yes, my dad was passionate about the military. His commitment was over-the-top. It was not unusual for him to work at his day job as a lawyer in Calgary during the week, take the red-eye flight to Ottawa on Friday night for a weekend of military work pertaining to DND (Department of National Defence) or NATO, return on the red-eye Sunday night, arrive in Calgary Monday morning and head straight to his law office from the airport. My dad was so busy with military activities that he didn't know what sports we played and had only a general impression of our friends. One time he made a rare phone call home and identified himself as Dad. "Dad who?" my brother asked. Which is all not to say my dad was a deadbeat or irresponsible in the least. He just operated in accordance with that unusual (at least in our neighbourhood), archaic value system: nation first, community second, family third. As a kid, I only wished he didn't have to be so obvious about it.

Uniforms throw people off. "Is your dad a pilot?" my friend from summer camp asked when she came for a visit. My parents told several stories of neighbours gently asking them if one of us kids was in any trouble, because when officers came over for a drink, it looked, to the uninitiated, as though the police had converged at our house. When my dad was picked up and delivered in a dark vehicle flying miniature Canadian flags and sporting a special licence plate, the rumour on the street was that the prime minister was visiting. Or Johnny Carson (quite a mystery how that one got started). Or that someone had died.

We had an annual Christmas visit from an entire busload of uniforms: the young carolling reservists. The singers would have visited the homes of several senior officers before our house, and they might have been served a drink or two at those homes. My dad generously and continuously topped up everyone's alcohol levels, sang along and, with a booming General voice, helped carry the tune. We kids were expected to attend the party, although in a perfunctory role. My parents never suggested that we mingle or make friends. I spent each carolling night refilling bowls of my mother's homemade nuts-and-bolts and avoiding conversation with these people who seemed not just drunk, but, again, from another planet. My siblings and I joked that our dad liked the army kids better than us, and I'm pretty sure that on those nights, he did. For us, it was an event to endure. For my dad and the carollers, it was fun. And when I look at in retrospect, I realize the evening wasn't so much about the booze or the carols as it was about "being army."

The Christmas-carolling drunk was always followed by the New Year's Day drunk: the levee. My dad's aide would arrive early, sometimes even before I left for skiing, and they would go to a service, then spend the day stopping at the Mess and as many legions as possible throughout the city. Late at night, Dad would be poured out of a military vehicle and into our house. Drunk, repetitive, reeking. None of us, not even my mother, would speak to him for a few days. And while I'll never condone the condition he came home in, I understand now why he felt it was important to have a drink with as many veterans, soldiers and reservists as possible during the levee. He didn't want the rank and file to see him as the kind of uppity officer who wouldn't have a drink with a regular soldier. And so his solution, apparently, was to have a drink with every one of them.

· · ·

These days, perhaps prompted by Canada's involvement in Afghanistan, it seems that the necessity, the very existence, of the military confuses people more than abbreviations and uniforms. Unless the Canadian Forces are in the headlines (i.e., unless members are dying), most civilians don't know what the army does. Parade? (My childhood view.) Shovel Toronto snow? (A popular western chestnut.) Keep the peace? (Peacekeeping is an activity civilians proudly believe requires no soldiering, just doll and candy delivery.) Civilians like me don't usually think of the Canadian Forces in Jerusalem or Khartoum or Sarajevo. In fact, somewhat like kids who don't know what their parents do, unless there's a crisis, we just don't think much about it at all.

My dad died at age 86 in 2005 and was given a grand send-off. Military colleagues helped him preplan the event, and I do mean "event," which included a flag-draped casket, pallbearers in full military dress, and the King's Own Calgary Regiment Band playing the "Colonel Bogey March." Everything but a parade. After the funeral, several of the guests commented that they'd never been to such a funeral. With all that pomp and circumstance, one friend said, my dad's funeral was like a scene from a novel.

At times, I do see my dad as a character from a novel, a kind of Dickensian figure. A one-dimensional, theatrical throwback. But thinking about him that way is a regression to my childhood. It is mixing up difference and superiority. As a child, I felt superior to those involved in the army. I felt superior to my father, to his interests, in a way that went beyond the usual embarrassment regarding parents. But then I grew up. Starting with superficial baby steps, such as realizing my friend who had a hot crush on a fighter pilot might not be out of her mind, and then gradually taking bigger steps, like noticing there were a large number of "normal," respectable people who were totally wowed by my dad and his commitment to, and support of, the military—actions made all the more impressive as they were during a time period when the Canadian Forces were often deemed unnecessary and, at least by me, really uncool. I've come a long way over the decades. Most recently, the son of one of my friends joined the military, and my first thought was "good on him."

As an adult, I don't feel superior to any military personnel, in the reserves or in the regular forces, be they my father or an anonymous Canadian. And whether I believe in a specific mission or not, I understand that soldiers commit their lives to their jobs based on values similar to my father's. Duty with honour. Service before self. Those are concepts I respect.

So once a year, if I am asked to present the Howard Trophy at the St. George's Day Parade and King's Own Calgary Regiment's birthday celebration, I will do it. I will feel honoured to have been asked. The trophy is a fitting tribute to my dad, and hopefully bears some meaning to the troop that earns it. But, no matter how hard I try, I will never fit in with the military crowd that gathers for chat and refreshments afterwards. Everyone in the Mess knows that I live on a different planet. Planet Civilian.

HOSTAGE TO FATE

Michael Hornburg

"Freedom is nothing else but a chance to be better."
—Albert Camus

On Remembrance Day 1980, when my first child was born, my father warned me that I had become a hostage to fate. Yet I still cried the first tears of joy in my life and willingly became a hostage of fate again when my son became my gift on Father's Day in 1983. With the birth of Rachel, Remembrance Day had shifted from a day that my job permitted me to only observe via radio to one of family parties, happiness and peace. Father's Day became a double celebration, as I received acknowledgement from my children and Nathan became another year older.

One of my greatest challenges as a young father came in the fall of 1988, when Nathan was enrolled in kindergarten. After only a few days, it became obvious that he was terribly unhappy, so I quit my job, took both kids out of school, and our family embarked on the process of home-schooling. This was not an easy decision to make for financial reasons, but stepping away from my symbolic and psychological role as provider in the family was even harder.

Our home-schooling program was only moderately successful in terms of structure, but it was profoundly rich in experience and memories. As we snuggled by the fire for hours on end, I would read aloud fantasy stories of mythic heroes and the eternal struggles between good and evil. And we would hike and ride our horses on the same ranch that the children's great-grandfather had established in the hills of southern Alberta in the late 1800s.

Fortunately, by the time the next school year began, Nathan's young cousin Katie and her mom had come to live with us, and Nathan was perfectly content to begin school with his cousin in the same class. I am certainly happy that little girls in Canada can freely go to school—for the sake of my daughter and my niece—and also because without the support of a little girl, perhaps Nathan might never have darkened the doorway of a school. From this youthful beginning, Nathan remained a lifelong best friend to his cousin and to many other girls and young women, and as a grown man he became a staunch defender of girls' rights to an education.

I returned to the fast-paced Calgary workforce, and so began for our family the rhythms and pleasures of a modern western Canadian life: the simple joys bound by the structure of the workday and the school year, meals and parties with friends, community projects and sports, and travel to visit my relatives in a bucolic oak forest with streams, ponds and cliffs west of St. Louis, Missouri. The kids did well in school and in sports, and when they became old enough they got summer jobs. Security and peace were issues I could take for granted.

Their mother home to look after them, the children grew to adulthood in their comfortable suburban home with a yard of many trees and gardens. All four grandparents survived until the children became adults. By the time Nathan was completing his second to last year of high school, the most serious issue was getting him motivated to get out of bed on time for his classes.

I often still read aloud to Nathan before bed during his high school years. The childhood tales of *The Hobbit, The Lord of the Rings* and *The Wonderful Wizard of Oz* gave way to Stephen Crane's "The Open Boat" and *The Red Badge of Courage* (which I thought was visceral and frightening, but Nathan said he found inspirational and challenging). I also read him several of Hemingway's stories of modern-day knights who fought battles on the side of the good and then died tragically in the struggle. These tales may have implanted a seed in Nathan's mind of the need for heroes even in our own time, because despite no military tradition on either side of his family, he began to talk about and research joining the Canadian Forces. Sometimes I wonder about other choices Nathan might have made and whether I could have influenced them differently, but I will never question sowing the ideas and choices born of great literature.

However, I do regret that because of our mutual passion for sports, I consented to the purchase of our household's first television early in 2001. This decision led to Nathan, his sister and me together witnessing the insanity and horror of 9/11 live on television. Along with the lives and ambitions of innumerable others, many aspects of my comfortable illusions were shattered that day, which occurred only three months after Nathan had made the first life-changing independent decision of his young adult life and joined the Armoured Corps

Reserves, the King's Own Calgary Regiment (KOCR), the week after his 18th birthday. Thus, just when the Western world had need of warriors, he had become a soldier.

• • •

From the first terrifying moments, I had the premonition that 9/11 would be a personal disaster for my family. Despite my anxiety, I could at least still go about my daily routine in Calgary if I chose to, but for a citizen soldier like Nathan, his routine took on a new urgency. Nathan had surprised me by embracing his warrior choice and new commitment, passing basic training with high marks due to his athleticism and belief in what he was doing and the teamwork of competing, suffering and learning with new friends.

The first Remembrance Day after the terrorists' attacks was a different experience for our family. Nathan's regiment paraded at The Military Museums, not far from our home in Calgary, and I went to watch him looking tall, handsome, strong and vital in his uniform, as much as to honour the solemnity of the occasion. For several years, this became my new November 11 routine: attend the service at the Museums, admire Nathan and his comrades on parade and then have a festive family birthday celebration for Rachel.

• • •

A couple of weeks after Remembrance Day in 2006, I received a phone call late at night from Nathan. He was by then a corporal (according to him and military lore "someone who worked for a living"), having always done well on the courses during his five years in the reserves. He had recently received his Arts and Science Certificate from

Mount Royal College and was working full-time before committing to more studies. One of his sergeants had just asked him if he would be willing to volunteer to do a tour of duty in Afghanistan. The assignment would be to learn to operate the recently acquired Leopard tanks that the Canadian Forces were going to begin deploying into theatre. He would be part of a small group from Calgary who would be the first reservists since the Korean War to serve on battle tanks in a war zone. We had talked briefly a few times before about him going on a mission, but it had always seemed abstract and not even necessarily connected to Afghanistan, although by then Afghanistan was always in the news and on our minds. I think because of my premonition, I refused to allow myself to think about him going there.

Nathan was by then 23 years old. To him, the future still looked far ahead and formless. He told me he wanted the adventure of going overseas on a tour and using his training to do something important. He wanted to be part of a team. He wanted to attain the highest goal possible for an armoured soldier—to operate a battle tank in combat. Most of all, he wanted to help girls and women and those oppressed. We didn't talk for long, but I was certainly not going to weigh in one way or another on a decision like this for him, so my advice was to sleep on it overnight.

He called back in about 20 minutes. He had also talked with a KOCR friend who said that if he didn't respond quickly, the military might simply go down their list and ask someone else. And so, despite being nervous, a bit worried and aware of the great risks—he did not want to be a hero, but he did want to be a man—he decided to accept the risks associated with that role and to go on the mission. (When reminded of the dangers of the mission by the Calgary media in interviews he did in the days before he left for Afghanistan, Nathan said, "That's all the more reason why someone like me should go.")

Settling his affairs to begin training took only a few days, but the training to operate a Leopard tank in a combat/war zone took nine months. Nathan was assigned to the regular Forces' Lord Strathcona's Horse regiment (Royal Canadians), based in Edmonton. He had to undergo the initial stigma of being the young reserve rookie fitting in with older, more experienced full-time soldiers, and he had to learn many new skills in a short, intensive period. He seemed to love most of it. He learned the mechanics necessary to service the tanks, and he travelled to New Brunswick, Texas, New Mexico and Germany to learn how to operate the tank in various terrains and to learn from the manufacturers. Throughout this time we kept our own conversations light and focused on the normal events and business of our daily lives. We remained private people and led our private lives. I think he was protecting me from the reality of his mission. He was beginning to grow wise.

• • •

When his training was over, his affairs organized and his goodbyes said, Nathan left at the end of August on a flight to Afghanistan. We talked about the future before he shipped out and we made plans as partners and friends. We had already bought a condominium together for him to live in, and we talked about selling it and buying another in a better part of town. We talked about travelling on adventures— maybe to hike in Hawaii or the southwest United States, or to take a road trip to the Midwest to visit family and friends—and we talked about maybe a small business or more schooling for him. All plans we could hope for in our world, the world he was leaving to help others with almost nothing to plan for in theirs.

Nathan made five phone calls to me in the brief time he was on his mission. On two of them, I was not home, so he left messages describing in guarded terms what he was doing, but never where. I wrote him weekly letters and they were serious and intense, but because of my enduring premonition from six years earlier and my superstitions arising from it, I refused to think about the dangers or the worst-case scenarios of anything happening to him. I thought that even the slightest hints of negativity might jinx him.

On the evening of September 22, 2007, he called from his Forward Operating Base (FOB). He was not specific, but he gave me details of a few incidents and I had a feeling that he was proud of his efforts and thought that he had the greatest friends, comrades and team that he could have hoped for. He also seemed nervous and indicated that things were a little more serious than he wanted to openly share with me. He had already seen the devastating effects of mortar shells coming into their base. (It wasn't until I read *FOB Doc*, by Dr. Ray Wiss, that I saw an actual photo of the shrapnel strike in the shower room that Nathan had alluded to. It had killed an Afghan interpreter.) Somehow, I still believed that a FOB was huge and impregnable and that the chance of any harm coming to Nathan was infinitesimally small, so I let it slide and kept up a steady chatter about all our favourite sports teams. Unfortunately, every one of them had lost in the preceding week, and things did not look good for their prospects. He did not comment much. No doubt, the fantasy world of sport was a less powerful stimulus for him at that time, but he let it be the substitute for worrying me with his reality. Nathan had done extremely well in his training. Too well, I reflect now. He had qualified to drive not just a Leopard tank, the battle tank, but the Armoured Recovery Vehicle, the ARV, with a crane on the front, not a cannon, and he accompanied every mission outside the wire. His job was to assist and rescue any vehicle or crew that became disabled in the rugged terrain.

The almost 12-hour time difference between the western part of Kandahar Province and Calgary meant he was calling early in the morning of his workday on September 23. A convoy had come in during the previous night: after he drank his coffee, he would go over and assist in the unloading with his ARV. He sounded relaxed and proud of that job, of working with real men and doing a real job in a dangerous, remote and hostile environment. He sounded mature, calm and healthy. Suddenly the phone cut out.

Within moments, he called again just to let me know that everything was still okay and that it was only a technical difficulty. He had to be on with his day, so I only had time to say, "I love you, son."

"I love you, too, Dad," he said as he hung up.

Those would be the last words we would ever speak to each other. The next day he went out on his last mission and to his last battle.

· · ·

On September 24, 2007, I went to work as usual, but a meeting kept me from returning home at my usual time. At about seven o'clock that evening, I had been home for only a few moments when my front doorbell rang. A visitor on an early Monday evening wasn't so very unusual; nevertheless, I had an eerie feeling and paused at my kitchen counter. I had a strong desire just to ignore the bell and remain standing there, but reluctantly, I answered the door and stepped into the moment that will now continuously mark the boundary between what was "before" and what will forever be "after." Three Canadian Forces officers stood at the door in full dress uniform and in that instant I knew, even before I heard the beyond horrible news, that my beloved only son, my perfect Father's Day gift, was lost to me forever.

The next days are not the clichéd blur, but full of innumerable powerful moments etched into my mind and spirit. A group of Nathan's closest family and our supporters went together to Trenton, Ontario, to welcome him home from that long journey from a dusty, worthless battlefield halfway around the globe. I had no expectations and was unprepared for the cast of dignitaries who joined us on the tarmac to pay their heartfelt and sincere respects. But I was even more unprepared for the trip back into Toronto along the Highway of Heroes. Nathan was the 71st Canadian soldier to die in Afghanistan and the first to travel along the highway after its name was officially changed and the new signs designating it as such were erected. To those thousands and thousands of people who turned out to pay their respects, I will forever be grateful. I have been angry during some stages of my life's journey, but I have never yet felt any anger over the loss of Nathan. Maybe it is because of the kindness of all those strangers.

There was an ominous sky over Trenton the afternoon when the Canadian Forces' Hercules aircraft brought Nathan home. It felt as if the skies would burst with rain at any moment. When our group went outside the hangar to see the coffin unloaded with solemn ceremony, the attendants paused with the flag-draped coffin for a moment at the side of the plane. At that very moment, a single, direct sunray broke through the threatening clouds and bathed the coffin in light. I closed my eyes and turned my face to the heavens. That image was captured on film and printed in the national newspapers. Immediately after the coffin was loaded into the hearse, the skies finally opened upon the crowd.

Those people of southern Ontario did not know that Nathan and his brothers-in-arms had been on a mission to open a police outpost when they were attacked. They did not know that the Canadian Forces had battled the Taliban for the better part of a day in a dry and rocky riverbed or that Nathan died after working for hours exposed to enemy fire from three directions as he aided in the successful rescue of a disabled tank and its crew. They did not know that Nathan died alone in his tank when it was hit by direct enemy fire—or that he would be awarded medals for his bravery and actions and some honorary distinctions that have been accorded to no other soldier in the Canadian Forces' history. To those who cheered Nathan that day in Ontario and again in Calgary on his parade from the airport and at his funeral and burial ceremony, he was simply Corporal Nathan Hornburg, a Canadian soldier doing what his country and his own nature asked of him, and a hero for that reason alone.

Crowds lined the streets of Nathan's processionals in Calgary, and an audience of 1,500 attended his funeral in the Roundup Centre on the Stampede grounds. I had nothing to compare this experience to, but it was an eternity of moments each of unbelievable power and emotion. At the interment, I said to our gathered family that I hoped this experience, this inconceivable loss of our most precious gift, would somehow make us better, not bitter. In hindsight, it must have been the kindness of all those strangers in both Ontario and Calgary that gave me the power, strength and insight to speak like this.

So many strangers, acquaintances and friends offered me condolences and solidarity. A very few have said unthinking and therefore insensitive things, but most have said profound words of sincerity and wisdom. A public death, a hero's death, touches many things in many people. I have often been told, "I can't imagine . . ." and I usually reply, "I can't either," because I still cannot. I often hear, "I am so sorry for your loss," but I have lost so little—compared to Nathan, who lost his life. I have lost my longtime answer of "never better" when asked how I am, but I have also gained so much: so many new friends and the opportunity to become conscious many times over of the potential dignity in the human experience. I know now that the world of grief is not mine alone—rather, it is the tragic glue of the world of humans.

The month after Nathan's October 4, 2007, funeral was my first Remembrance Day without him. I went to The Military Museums and remembered and truly grieved for the first time as one with the crowd. I had never told Nathan that when he was on parade with his regiment, I had a hard time singling him out from the other soldiers despite the fact that he was among the tallest. Now this was a strange comfort to me. He could be one of the tall, proud soldiers still standing at attention.

• • •

In 2008, when a small group of organizers decided to honour Nathan with a memorial run on Father's Day, I became aware of one young woman who seemed to be doing an exceptional amount of individual fundraising and promotion. I asked her if she had been a close friend of Nathan and she said, "No. I only met him briefly once or twice before we happened to be at the same party on New Year's Eve at a fancy home with a swimming pool. During the party, a bunch of guys started grabbing people and throwing them into the pool. I didn't know many people there and I had on my good clothes, and I didn't want to be thrown in. They grabbed me and started dragging me toward the pool. I was crying and looking at the crowd of strangers, when suddenly this one guy stepped out and said, 'Hey, guys, she said she doesn't want to go into the pool and she isn't going in.'"

Of course, that guy who stepped out of a crowd to stand up for a stranger, a young woman, was Nathan, and my eyes welled with tears when she told me that story. He was the guy willing to take a risk and to do the right thing. He dared to be brave, and on that night he got away with it.

Before the memorial run, I was asked to attend a military ceremony at the base in Edmonton, during which the entire battalion was honouring Nathan and Michael Hayakaze, the other member of the regiment who lost his young life during that tour of duty. I was belatedly and hurriedly on my way up the highway to the service when I learned that I was expected to go onstage and say a few words. Previous to this, my entire public speaking career had consisted of a few emotional words to a small group in a community hall—and that time, I had prepared a topic and had spoken from notes. Fortunately, this young woman's story—a true parable and a fitting metaphor for the Canadian Forces' Afghan mission—came to my mind and I delivered my speech without breaking down. I felt Nathan at my shoulder that day.

• • •

A few weeks after Nathan's funeral, my daughter's doctor confirmed her first pregnancy. Nine months from his conception date, (September 24, 2007, the exact date of Nathan's death) my first grandchild was born with many of the same newborn features as his uncle. The mysterious movements of the Universe?

. . .

After we lost Nathan, we discovered some of his own words on his computer. He wrote,

> I know that war is terrible. War involves death, and death involves pain, both for the deceased and for the deceased's acquaintances, but more people will be born, and with each generation the world will seem a little smaller, and be a little closer to being healed. Unfortunately, healing is often a painful process and loss is often involved, whether this is a loss of life or the loss of hope. However, it is the death of hope, not the death of people that is actually a stinging blow to our planet.

The loss of a child is a very humbling experience. So many hopes, ambitions and expectations suddenly vanish. Even though I often just want my private reality back, I have chosen to remain "public" after the loss of my child by continuing to speak before groups, and this is another of the huge changes in my Remembrance Day experiences. The innumerable and constant wars require their heroes to fight on the side of the good, the oppressed and the weak, and they need witnesses to remember and recount their deeds. They require someone to tell the tale, to keep the story alive, to keep each generation hopeful that every war might be the last.

Perhaps this is Nathan's greatest gift to me. He has made me a storyteller. Perhaps this is how I can keep him real to me. This is why Remembrance Day is so important to me now. This is my chance—this is *our* chance—to be better, not bitter. This is the fate to which I am a willing hostage.

Peace.

RECONSTRUCTION TOUR

Scott Waters

While the other patio dwellers bask in Winnipeg's fleeting summer sun, Paul and I hash out his time in the Balkans. He seems to be thinking out loud when he tells me, "There was such hate over there and you know, that stuff ain't easy to reconcile. I guess I need to believe in evil as a tangible entity, like an oiliness working its way around the planet. I mean how the hell else do I explain what happened?"

As Paul continues his Croatian anecdotes and tries to disassemble that region's ethnic hostility, I've become preoccupied waiting for Ian's arrival. I wonder whether I'll be able to recognize Ian's disguise 17 years in the making. Even though we haven't seen each other since the end of the Cold War, I tell myself I'll easily pass this test. And of course there's the question of his personality—will Ian have changed since our time together or will he arrive encased in a time capsule? Paul and I have discussed our respective and relatively successful drives to reinvent ourselves, and so someone like Ian, who chose to stay in the infantry for 20 years, stands as a manifestation of our own rejections.

Until his arrival, however, Paul and I enjoy our pints, talk about the collapse of the Balkans and Paul's participation in it. He summarizes his thoughts regarding the indelibility of evil, "How the fuck can people hold a grudge for a thousand years?"

The three of us served in the same battalion and rifle company, but owing to differing enlistment dates and positions, Ian and Paul don't actually know each other. There are, however, numerous nostalgic entry points for them to get acquainted by: the hilarity of drunken fights at bars near our base in Victoria, BC; that city's ubiquitous rain; sodden exercises in the rain; and, importantly, a UN tour in Croatia. As Ian and Paul are both dealing with the fallout of their experiences, the tour offers their most loaded intersection and the reason for this low hum of anticipation.

Ian shows up a half-pint later, and with a focused lope he crosses the patio. Closing my part of the gap, I hug the man hiding inside these years of distance. Ian's shades float high on wild brown locks that were kept short during my years with him. His mop also frames pink cheeks and slightly wrinkled eyes. The smile has remained a constant—not shown without reason but as genuine as ever, though now it seems slightly alloyed. While he's put weight on, I've lost it, and as summation of that, apropos of nothing else, he suggests, "Maybe you got the HIV." His joking suggestion that I have AIDS takes a moment to uncomfortably settle in, and I recognize he's a little suspicious of the artist I chose to become. Ian orders a Blue (another constant) and the three of us hang out a couple of pints longer than we had planned. To the folk clustered at tables around us, we're casual in our catching up.

For Paul, though, this is anything but. He's worked hard to filter the doubts and resentments grown full during his tour in Croatia, and this is the first time in a long time that he's talked shop and unpacked his infantry persona. While they sport similar haircuts, golf shirts and sunglasses, Ian seems defined by a laissez-faire demeanour, while Paul's air hints at someone off-centre and unsure. Weeks later he would tell me of his conflicted feelings during our pints with Ian, but for now we just catch up, laugh, complain about our knees and avoid topics tucked in our shirt pockets.

Eventually it's time for Paul to walk back to his life, his wife and his Jack Russell, and for me to be handed off to Ian—to step once more into a past I'd also run away from.

As institutions have defined my adult life, the last couple of weeks have seen me bussing it around the Prairies, visiting old university and army buddies, and Ian is the last stop on this reunion tour. Though really just a matter of logistics as I make my way east, he is the perfect full stop to these interludes, these August bullet points.

• • •

The next morning, mildly hungover, I suggest to Ian that we go grab a coffee and shoot the poop. When back home in west-end Toronto, coffee culture is how I would navigate the first half of the day, but to Ian I might as well have suggested we go feed ducks. Just as I'm preoccupied with Ian's evolution I'm also trying to see my own metamorphosis: to consider what remains constant and what has turned, and my love of a good Americano is certainly one turn. It's not that Ian doesn't partake in caffeine, but neither is it a social tool for him. "Uh, coffee . . . ? Well, how 'bout we go grab a beer and shoot some stick instead?" These days I suck at pool but happily agree to replay the old role. This is why I'm here in the Prairies.

Having slogged through both basic training and battle school, we'd been sent to our regiment's 3rd Battalion and posted to the same platoon. I was a little bit of an odd duck, with music and reading choices that didn't sit quite right with some of the other grunts. In this, Paul and I were kindred spirits, listening to Camper Van Beethoven and the Pixies when Merle Haggard and BTO were the norm. As for Ian, even back then he flew the hoser flag, but the army excels at creating unlikely friendships through tribulation, and so I came to count him as solid—a committed soldier and drinking buddy. But all good things crumble under their own weight, and after my three-year contract with the infantry I'd cartwheeled away from our shared life, opting to join the mass exodus of disaffected grunts seeking some sort of new start in the Okanagan Valley: retiring to beaches, fishing trips, rain-free winters, the bliss of pogey and, for me, an eventual university degree in visual arts. Ian and the other lifers were left to their pragmatic jingoism of complaining and of training to fight, of the insular, inverted society I'd developed a burning hatred for.

If you're a young soldier, returning to civvy life equals a failure—an inability to hack army life. If you become a civvy and get back in, well then you're guilty of the opposite—unable to fend for yourself, a loser who can't cook his own meals or pay his own bills. One of the benefits of our mass immigration to Kelowna was that we constituted a sort of support system. When the wage-slave life seemed a bit too demeaning and pointless, we were there to talk the vulnerable out of returning to the infantry's gruffly welcoming bosom. So when I say that Ian had a short, failed attempt at civvy life in the mid-nineties, recognize that "failure" is a subjective and inescapable Catch-22. With the exception of that blip, he'd stayed hard-core, stayed infantry or recce. There are some great photos from his tour in Afghanistan, up in the mountains or in ravines with eyes blacked out by a rectangle reserved for those serious enough to not be fucked with—the anonymous elite of reconnaissance. Those shots, though, they represent the myth society feeds on and the same myth that compelled many of us to enlist in the army out of high school. The myth covers torn ligaments and disintegrated cartilage, compressed vertebrae and the emotional damage that is the permanent reward for being a combat soldier. This is the legacy that matters and the one Ian lives with.

The Brunswick (the 'Wick to the locals) is as awesome a joint as it is a damning indictment of redneck rye-and-Coke Canadiana. Walking through the cold beer store to the bar, we also pass pale, luminous banks of VLTs, casting their numbing glow onto middle-aged residents. Tattered pool tables are our destination, though, not the fake promise of financial emancipation; we prefer the fleeting, radiant banality of brews and cues. Ian orders a Blue, then raises an eyebrow as I ask the waitress, "What do you have in a medium-dark ale?" Keith's Amber is the entirely reasonable answer I should have known enough to just ask for by name.

I'm jealous of Ian's casual ease with the other bar-goers. Though they're strangers to each other, there's nonetheless a covenant of familiar accessibility that I haven't known in years. Like a stop on a pilgrimage to nowhere in particular, the bar-goers—drinkers, pool players and gamblers alike—acknowledge each other's journey. By way of playful banter, Ian offers to the emaciated barstool–Kenny Rogers, "You don't wanna fuck with us; we were soldiers." This flatters me and substantiates the age-old promise of once a soldier, always a soldier. Four tours in the Balkans and one in Afghanistan make Ian a soldier, whereas I just tried it out. Over the years, the booze and debauchery of my "service" has come to define my artistic practice, so while the infantry tinted my life, I've also made good use of those years. Being a grunt, however, has forever altered Ian's core being, and his inclusion of me into the ranks of the damaged combat soldier is something I am silently thankful for—it is an admittance into the mythology of soldiering for which I am not qualified.

While the banter bounces around, I'm reminded of something Paul and I had discussed a few days ago. Walking south along the Red River, we attempted to locate our place in the infantry. Paul was always more of a skeptic and needed escape on the weekends, going so far as to hang out at Victoria's gay bar—as far from army culture as you could get. But in addition to the reg force years, he also did a haul in the militia. In short, he was more wary and I more hell-bent, but maybe that applied to being a civvy as well. Ian, however, seemingly always believed. Certainly he wears the contradictory but necessary skepticism of a career grunt.

Playing the old parts here at the 'Wick, Ian rouses the rabble, with me as his happy sidekick. As he racks, Ian reminds me that back in our days together, he did nothing on the weekends that might be construed as separation from the bubble. While some went camping, hiking or driving up island to check out the hippies and surfers at Jordan River, he played it close, drinking and watching movies, going out for pizza perhaps; there was enough camping on the job, enough hiking to fill a centenary. Ian's public persona was always tied to the job, just like here at the pool table. I'm sure there'd be no dragging him to an art gallery or duck pond, just as there's no venturing out for an Americano or iced cappuccino for the sake of socialization. Coffee drinking is done in the

FOB, the patrol base or the company HQ, not on the weekend or in retirement.

What I come to realize is that Ian is negotiating two personalities. The portrait side of his coin is this slightly jovial, slightly confrontational shaggy-haired pool player. This is the soldier archetype. After a life spent on the line and now retired, he wants folk to know he served well and to treat him with the cautious respect that one affords the aging caribou found on the backside of his coin. We play pool (I only win on a scratch) and drink our respective brews. Our time is easy and comfortable, playful and macho, like the years passed have been only days or weeks. But I know this persona is the equivalent of an armoured vest.

There's a truth in what the movies proclaim—army friends are friends apart—and I'll drift into hyperbole by saying such friendships are indelible and almost sacred. All other friendships are shadows cast by the light of grunts. But as deep as our friendship is, it's also cautious. I still love Ian, but we are obviously circling around something other than the pool table.

A few years after I got out of the army, a friend in art school took on a serious tone and asked me, "Have you ever killed anyone?" Taken aback, I was also . . . well, flattered. Here, though, pint in one hand, stick in the other, I won't ask; I want Ian to tell me of damage and trauma. Killing. But I know better and care more. I won't go diving in, but the topic is certainly a tickle in my throat and is where our friendship meets its test. I won't ask but I hope I'm trusted enough for him to open up. And Ian, I suspect, needs to consider whether the ease of our reacquainting is equal to the degree of trust required.

Later, as we sit around in his living room drinking rum and Coke, Ian's pool-hall persona cedes to the other—the damaged—one, as his shoebox of deployment photos is brought out. Compiled in no order, these years of moments are Ian in a box. The stack reminds me of a passage from Alex Garland's *The Beach*, where the narrator talks of not taking photos because those documented moments force out the equally important ones that didn't benefit from a handy camera. I wonder if this can be the case here. Surely there is permanence to Ian's witnessing, and all the photos can accomplish is to partially bridge the gap between our lives.

Regardless of the photos' function, I am complimented again by this trust and I hope he knows it. Sipping my syrupy highball, I'm also nursing my guilt at feeling this voyeuristic excitement. Tucking the guilt away, I believe I'm also helping him deal with the hairline fissures of his life, and for that reason I am happy to glimpse down into the shallow depth of the shoebox. Singling out an image, Ian passes it over. From inside a Croatian school gym there are passive but obvious signs of what can only be called an execution. "What was harder, the Balkans or Af'stan?" is all I can figure out to ask. There is a certainty equal to the difficulty Ian has with his words. "Croatia. There was no fucking humanity left in that country."

We pause and have a drink in heavy silence. I stare into the photo, scuff marks on the floor. A horizontal web of fractured plaster makes its way toward a haphazard row of holes at too low a point along the wall. The basketball hoop remains, untouched and indifferent.

Placing the photo in the tidy pile next to the shoebox, we move on to images with easier topics: guys cheating at euchre, APCs in Croatia. We spend some time chuckling over Paul's sinking of an APC at a creek crossing and at how the Jordanian peacekeepers would sell their diesel to the Croats in exchange for food. We ride these waves for a while, turning our conversation to old friends happy in their lives but also to friends dead and missing, amputated and scarred. These tensions are broken by honest but slightly forced jocularities.

"Yeah, Brydon told me about getting high on cough syrup when he was a civvy and codeine was still the active ingredient. We did this Ex. in Wainwright—you know the one where we drove for the militia and those part-timers got all fucked up in the LAV crash? Anyway, Brydon and I were getting wasted in the booze tent and pissing onto the dirt so we wouldn't have to try and stand."

Ian gets to the point, "Fuck, I miss that guy."

I didn't know they were also good friends and so it comes as a shock to hear that the super-easygoing Brydon has "gone to ground" and is unreachable. Not a trace has been seen or heard since he got out in the wake of another mutual friend's suicide while they were deployed. We both suspect he might have gone back to Ontario, his home before he knew soldiering, but there's no way to know. Brydon is a cotter pin absent from Ian's life, and I realize that I'm acting as lesser substitute for our missing friend. This role, though, is one I'm comfortable with. It is my rightful position on the ladder of army friends, a friend who was there at the beginning but not through the hard years.

A few days after getting home, I look at my own photos of Brydon in my own shoebox and see a kid with boots too big and combat shirt a little on the baggy side, but with a contagious smile and a good knowledge of the Ontario punk scene.

• • •

Out of the army a couple of years now, Ian spent some time tiling kitchens and bathrooms. Not surprisingly, that dip into the drudgery of workaday life couldn't hold, but now, surprisingly, he's writing screenplays. I'd heard this was the case and was eager to maybe talk about the craft and check out his production. As it turns out, the screenplays centre on the antics of the squirrels in his backyard. It would be easy for me to get down on him for passing up such fecund experiences as his, but I think back to something the artist Gertrude Kearns wrote, that your increasing proximity to trauma often equals your unwillingness to depict it. This is, I expect, where Ian currently resides.

As I sit here and type, I like to think of him with a rum and Coke by the keyboard, clicking at the keys and pausing for a sip and a rub of his chin—I hope this is the case.

• • •

There is a wreck in your head, part of the aftermath, and you must dismantle the wreck. But after many years you discover that you cannot dismantle the wreck, so you move it around and bury it.
—Anthony Swofford, *Jarhead*

The military memoir has surged of late and many are raw and vengeful, words assembled as attempts to dismantle demons and create some semblance of forward momentum on the part of the authors. Maybe I'm assigning a single trajectory when there are as many motivations as there are authors, but Ian's squirrels make me think he's running hard and fast away from his wreck, not yet ready to attempt a dismantling. That's not it either, though. Just as most soldiers are unwilling to attach the title "hero" to their actions, most are also reluctant to allow reporters and artists to diffuse their personal struggles.

Am I doing Ian a service with the words written here? Perhaps all he wants is to move on, to reclaim some echo of a world prior to having his eyes forced opened. Perhaps all he wants is to type his way back into a world where a squirrel's gravity-bending leap from porch to apple tree will be the most astonishing feat of the day.

. . .

Eventually the rum, the gin and the Blue are drained and we call it a night. The morning comes quickly and another sunny day sidles up, finding me foggy and rumpled. It's all over, though. Today I'll catch my flight back to the present, away from this reunion tour. Tomorrow, unbelievably, I'll be back to my routine of part-time teaching and full-time painting. After I pack up my shaving tackle, Ian drives me counter-clockwise across town, past Winnipeg's old and now abandoned Kapyong Barracks. He points out the headquarters for the local Rifle companies, as well as the recce, ADP and Assault Pioneer buildings, and I have the sense of moving through a wormhole in a RAV4. My thoughts are on the derelict architecture of the base and on my friend as we navigate some very sludgy time and space. The wide intersections, traffic lights and aging malls pass by as the city thins out, and we use these waning minutes to squeeze in what we can about the future. I'll be returning to Winnipeg at the same time next summer, so we start talking about a larger reunion, a gathering of various odd-balls who were once thrown together and eventually detached from each other. It's a reunion that would invariably include brews and cues, outrageous tales and maybe the odd flying fist. Before pulling into the airport, we pass the pristine new Greyhound terminal. This was my arrival point a few days back and is a counterpoint to the barracks. The city seems rooted in my past, and it is these transitional spaces at its periphery, the bus terminal, the airport, which stand for my present. Ian and I pull into the terminal at YWG and whether it's to avoid a parking ticket or an awkward emotional departure, he guns it into the departures entrance and I jump out in a classic combat unload.

"Great to see you."

"Yeah, you too man."

FINDING MY WAY BACK TO SOME KIND OF NORMAL

Jill Kruse

It wasn't an easy Christmas to begin with. For the first time ever, we were trying to celebrate without my husband, Greg, at home. This move to Pembroke was also our first posting, far from our home in New Brunswick. Other military families were doing the same thing, I kept telling myself. I could do this, too: just keep putting one foot in front of the other, keep busy, keep the kids busy and we'd all get through it.

Christmas Eve arrived and we did pretty well. My 11-year-old daughter, Kari, and I managed to put together a quick dinner of our favourite finger food before the seven o'clock church service. Six-year-old twins Megan and Victoria were precious in the Christmas Eve pageant: the cutest little wise men you ever saw. After getting the girls to bed, I managed to get all the presents wrapped and under the tree: playing Santa without my usual helper.

By midnight, I was sitting by the phone with a glass of wine and Greg's present before me—the one he thoughtfully had delivered by one of his army buddies just a few days before. By 12:30, I had decided he wasn't going to call, so I opened my present. It was the beautiful blue sapphire and diamond necklace I tried on months before, never dreaming I'd ever get it. Jewellery never seemed that important to me; there were always other things we needed. We'd been on a date and visiting a jewellery store in the Pembroke Mall just before he deployed, and he had given me the matching sapphire earrings as my birthday gift. The necklace reminded me of how our date didn't quite go as either of us expected. I had burst into tears at the restaurant when he said he didn't think we could plan a special vacation like a trip to Disneyland on his return from the war, because he wasn't sure what shape he'd be in. All I could think was, didn't he get it? Didn't he understand how hard this was going to be for me and the girls? Waiting, wondering if he would make it . . . home.

As I put my precious necklace aside, I decided the call wasn't coming and I had better get some rest for the morning. I reminded myself that with the nine-hour time difference and the fact that it was Christmas, he may not have been able to call. I learned later that he had called his mom instead: something he always did at midnight on Christmas Eve. And I am thankful he did, now; it was such a gift to her.

• • •

On Christmas morning the girls did what they always did: woke up early, oohed and ahhed over gifts and fought over who got to open the next one. We took a video so Daddy could see how well his girls managed Christmas without him. I imagined how he would laugh when he watched our yellow Lab, Pal, rip open his Christmas gifts.

When Greg finally did call that morning, I thought it was a better present than the necklace. I passed the phone between all three girls so they could each tell him about their Christmas and ask him how he liked the ornaments and gifts we had sent him. After about 20 minutes I got another chance to hear his voice.

He asked, "So what do you want to do this summer when I get back?" Since he'd already told me Disney was out of the question, I said, hopefully and with some resignation, "I think we should use the extra pay from the tour to fix up the Kruse family camp." (We loved the place in Gaspé more than anything; it was our honeymoon spot.) "Well," he said, "I don't think that's gonna happen."

My heart sank . . . again. "Why not?" I asked, bracing for bad news, certain he was going to tell me that the army had extended his tour and that he wouldn't be home till summer, or worse, fall.

"Because we're going *home*!"

He explained that he had received his posting message and we were to be posted back home in New Brunswick to Base Gagetown; he had been assigned to teach at the Armoured School.

Well, you have never heard anything like the squeal of delight that came out of me that morning. The girls all came running, their eyes full of excitement. "Girls! We are going home! Daddy's been posted home!" This was, without a doubt, the best news, and very best present, I could ever have hoped for.

I told him how I'd asked one of his superiors at the Engineers' Christmas party whether there were any possible postings to Gagetown. Regimental Sergeant Major Pynn had looked at me with a glint in his eye, saying only, "Maybe." I learned later that Greg had known for weeks but was waiting to tell us on Christmas Day. I am still amazed how he kept this wonderful news a secret.

"Don't be talking to anyone; nothing is official yet!" he warned me.

I managed to squeak out "okay" and "I love you" before saying goodbye, but later, at the free Christmas dinner for military families on deployment at a restaurant near the base, I sashayed from table to table, exclaiming, "I'm going home, I'm going home!" No one could burst my happy bubble that day.

• • •

On Saturday morning, a day and two nights after getting the news about going home, I was on the computer, checking in with friends on Facebook. I could hear the girls watching the cartoon version of *Anne of Green Gables*. When the doorbell rang, I looked at Kari and said: "We are not expecting anyone or anything; we have all our presents." But I still hoped it would be our kind mailman, who delivered belated Christmas parcels even on Saturdays.

Then, as my mind turned to another possibility, one I wanted to immediately dismiss, my heart started pounding. I had a very bad feeling! I DID NOT WANT TO OPEN THAT DOOR.

Whoever was there was not going to leave. I slowly got up from the computer and because I was still in my pyjamas, I went to the closet to grab my coat. Fearfully opening the inside door, I gazed down toward the garage door and was horrified to see through the window—the uniforms, the distraught faces.

"No, no, no!" I whispered, begging, "Please tell me he's just hurt, please tell me he's just hurt." As I descended down those few steps in what felt like slow motion, I hoped beyond hope that they would tell me Greg was NOT DEAD: anything, anything but that.

I peered into the brown eyes of my padre, the man who—just two nights earlier—had stood with me and discussed the why of the war and our reasons for battle: "If not us, then who?" he had asked. "Evil such as this needs to be overcome." And the two of us agreed that the kind of evil happening in Afghanistan was the variety no one wanted and good soldiers fought against.

Now, looking at me, he said nothing. While the young military engineer with him said those dreadful words, "I regret to inform you . . ." Padre Bob just shook his head as if thinking, what terrible news to have to bring to his parishioner at Christmas. As I look back at that moment now and recall the seconds before the world as we knew it changed, I wonder how I ever found the courage to open the door.

• • •

My friend Cyndi and I had once discussed the awful possibility. I think every deployed spouse has to think about it at some point. I told her that if they ever came to my door, I would run. And I did try to run. I made it as far as our bedroom when I realized I had totally forgotten about the children. Horrified that I had left them alone to face this military assault, I raced down the stairs to the living room, pulled my bewildered girls close to me and announced tearfully: "Daddy is not coming home ever again. Daddy is dead!" I will never forget the look on their little faces the moment I broke their hearts.

I can't really describe the rest of that awful day. I was attached to the phone for eight hours straight, with dreaded calls to his mother, a widow herself, and to my elderly mom, who had prayed daily on her rosary for his safety. But somehow, I bore what I was sure would kill me. I had no choice: I had three little girls who needed me.

With the help of my mother, whose faith astounds me; nine brothers and sisters, whose love and prayers carried me; my military family, particularly my good friend Cyndi, who got me through the worst of it; my assisting officer, Dan; Padre Bob; the faithful regimental leaders of 2CER; my mother-in-law, Penelope; her sons, Christian and Tim; and countless others whose love and prayers held me together, somehow I managed to plan a funeral, attend too many ceremonies, and watch in agony and defeat as they carried my beloved to his final resting place.

For the first few days and even months following the horrid notification, there were times I denied my new reality. It had to be a mistake; I could not be a widow. I dreamed Greg was alive. He came to me and held me; I awoke feeling him beside me, his hand in mine. I could visualize him alive in front of me anytime, day or night—for weeks, maybe months. My military friends were still waiting for their spouses to come home from the same tour. The visualization I had used whenever I got nervous on deployment was to imagine him on the big white bus he left on and tell myself: he is on the bus . . . he is on his way home to us. Now I realize I will never see that bus.

• • •

I felt guilty about not waking up the moment Greg died. He died at approximately 12:30 PM Afghanistan time or 3:00 AM my local time. For months, and still during stressful times now, I awake around 3:00 AM. I just cannot fathom that I slept while my beloved was murdered, his body exploding across the cruel sands of the Panjwaii district of Afghanistan.

In addition to this constant life-sucking pain in my heart, I was angry. Angry about the war that took my husband. Angry that he was never coming home and deployment was now permanent. Angry that my children would never have their father, ever again. Angry that we did not have enough time on this earth as husband and wife. (We had just celebrated our 12th wedding anniversary before he left.) Angry that all of our hopes and dreams were gone. Angry at the cowardly and deadly tactics of the evil Taliban.

My worst time of day was when the girls arrived home from school. The idea of helping with homework, preparing meals, acting like it was a normal day, was monumental to me. Sometimes the smallest thing could set me off. I would start ranting: "I hate this, I hate my life!" Then I would hate myself for not being the kind of mother my children needed and deserved, the mother I was before Greg was killed.

I wrote in my journal:

I used to believe that if I did everything right, I would get my happy ending. If I just prayed the right way, made the right amount of money, took care of my body, went back to church, took good care of my babies . . . well, it would all turn out okay. I believed it with my heart and my soul . . . And every day I said prayers of thanksgiving, not just once a year: every single day. I had exactly what I wanted: a man I loved like crazy. Together we made a family of three beautiful little girls. I did not take this for granted. I knew this was my pot of gold.

Processing the death of the one you love is long and torturous. One of my coping mechanisms was eating. I probably ate every

20 minutes for the first two weeks. Of course the food left my body almost as quickly. Strangely, I also managed to get at least six hours of sleep pretty regularly. Somehow I would just shut down, thank God. I still had to manage our home, take care of our girls, get them to school each morning, help with homework, make meals and get ready to sell the house in the spring. We were still moving "home" as planned.

Eventually, I realized that if I was ever going to survive this and help my children get through this, I needed help to find my way back to some kind of normal. At first, I looked for someone to help my children cope with the loss of their father. The Phoenix Centre in Petawawa specializes in helping children and military families cope with all kinds of issues. It took weeks, but I finally got a call back from a counsellor. Elizabeth was a godsend. Instead of helping the girls, she understood I needed help first, so I met with her weekly. Within a month I was managing to get through the day without losing it. The children and I met with her only about four times, because Elizabeth and I realized that if I was given the opportunity to vent and sort out my emotional turmoil, then the children would be okay. Just knowing I had someone to call when things got tough was a relief.

There were so many things I had to come to terms with. This was no longer deployment where all the tasks I managed were temporary. I was now responsible for everything, forever. That predicament overwhelmed me daily. Yes, now I was like any single mom; I had to do things on my own. But, unlike many single moms, I also had resources to draw upon. Thanks to the life insurance and the death benefits and income support provided by the military and Veteran Affairs, I had the financial means to hire help. So I hired people to clean the house and get it ready for the market. I hired a woman to help the twins with homework. I told myself

I did not have to prepare every meal. I decided I could do whatever I needed to do to get myself through the worst time of my life as long as it was not drugs, alcohol or any other detrimental substance or practice.

• • •

When the girls finished school that June, we made the emotionally difficult trip back to New Brunswick (with the urn of Greg's ashes riding shotgun). Although I was looking forward to going home, our house was over 30 years old, so I decided to use some of the money to do upgrades and try to make it my own now. The summer before Greg deployed, we had discussed replacing the roof, so I did this and had the inside repainted after the tenants left. I also lined up a friend to build a new deck in our backyard. I had the eavestroughs replaced, a stone walkway installed, the old crumbling driveway repaved and an above-ground pool installed. Eventually, my financial advisor told me I had better stop or I would soon have no savings for the future.

Despite all the cosmetic changes, I felt dissatisfied. I was unable to recreate what we once had, that feeling of being home. As much as I wanted to come home and renew our ties with our neighbours and friends, it was not the same and would never be the same again—for me or my girls. Greg was not home with us. There are memories and reminders of the life we had and the life we dreamed of everywhere. Not just in our home, but in our neighbourhood and city: the parks we took the kids to, the nightclub where we met, the restaurants we went to on date nights.

There are places I am still stuck. There are still boxes unpacked, books unshelved and pictures waiting to be hung. My bedroom has been beautifully refurnished but the walls are still bare. The tributes and military medals await a wall of honour. I know I will get there, someday. Taking care of myself, emotionally and physically, and my girls: that has to be my priority now. I am seeing a grief therapist who has helped me find my road to recovery and independence. I am beginning to find my joy again. I have rediscovered my passion for tennis, and when the weather permits, you'll find me on the courts taking all my frustration out on that little yellow ball. I also have someone special in my life now who has allowed me the time and space to grieve, helping me through a very difficult time. He is handy, too, and often takes care of those chores I would have depended on Greg for. I have often said Greg sent him to me. I don't know what the future looks like yet, but there are more days where I am okay with that than not. One step at a time, I will get back to "my kind of normal."

And I can now say that despite our great loss, we are blessed. I am blessed to have known such a wonderful and loving man, who gave me sapphires and diamonds, which I now treasure and wear at memorials and other special occasions. The girls are blessed to have known such a loving and devoted father. I am blessed with the task of raising these three beautiful girls; blessed that I can call and chat with my wise and wonderful mother, who turned 90 last July. Blessed to have so many good and loyal friends, devoted brothers and sisters, Greg's comrades and family who check in from time to time, a dog who won't leave my side, kind and helpful neighbours, and sufficient income to support us as we make this difficult journey without our Greg.

Till we meet again, my love. CHIMO. PEACE. LOVE.

For my beloved Greg, who never wanted to burst my happiness bubble, and our three beautiful young ladies, who gave me back my hope and my life.

THE PERILS OF WAR
AND MOTHER–SON RELATIONSHIPS

Joan Dixon

"It's a tradition," my 17-year-old son informed me. He wasn't exactly asking for permission; the tattoo could have been a *fait accompli* before I ever—if I ever—saw it. He was willing me to say, "It's your body, your choice," just as I had said to his sister when she'd considered multiple piercings many years earlier. Even if I'd wanted to risk hypocrisy or discourage him from confiding in me about his future plans, I knew it would be impossible to change his mind. I'd always had to pick my battles.

The idea of a tattoo didn't seem battle-worthy to me, but the design Nik chose—a Canadian flag etched in military green—represented different things to each of us. To him, it signified his most recent and significant accomplishment: he'd survived basic training. To me, the green flag symbolized the Canadian Forces' successful recruitment of my son, who—up until now—had never been easily co-opted. How did this happen?

A decade earlier, when my children were younger and my patience exasperated, the worst thing I could threaten them with was military school. I was joking then, but now, the joke's on me. Instead of simply helping my son with his choice of university in his last year of high school, I found myself evaluating a much bigger decision regarding his future: he wanted to be a soldier.

Granted, mothers have been losing sons to the army since time immemorial. In some countries, military service is still compulsory for youth, and perhaps it's an appropriate rite of passage to adulthood, especially given the dubious life choices some "kidults" or "adultescents" make. But I hadn't seen the army coming for my son.

No career soldiers in either branch of my family supplied the tradition or heritage. Long after escaping from war-torn east Europe, my father-in-law still regularly vocalizes his deep antipathy to soldiering. Like most of his peers, my own father had traded his youth to the RCAF during the Second World War, and my Norwegian mother had bravely resisted her country's military occupation, but both had essentially entombed their experiences. (Mum, however, could never stand her children wearing military green, so I can't imagine what she'd think of her grandson's tattoo.)

My own closest brush with soldiers came during the FLQ bomb threats in Montreal in 1970, when we were routinely sent from school to the local armoury. As much as they were there to protect us, the uniforms and guns in our community scared us more. I grew up in the time of *Make Love, Not War*, and like most of my generation I was appalled about Vietnam. War was anachronistic to us. Only later, when we could think of soldiers as peacekeepers rather than warriors, did the military become more respectable in our minds, although still not high on our radar. These days, many Canadians still seem ambivalent or dismissive—half of us want to close our eyes and hope someone else deals with our defence and the rest of the world's issues.

Having a son of military age with a war going on crystallized the debate for me: the theoretical suddenly slammed into the reality. Even if we both believed that living in a democracy means sharing in its burdens, Nik insisted on walking the talk. He was far more informed and engaged than I had been at his stage, about to graduate from high school with both citizenship and academic honours, yet I considered him an unfinished kid with so many options. He wanted to make a life-altering decision that—without truly understanding all the reasons why—I felt less than enthusiastic about. I had never considered myself a worrier or a helicopter parent, but I also never foresaw my son as potential IED fodder.

Looking back, there were some hints: Nik had often played soldier while camouflaged in the woods outside our home; he constructed forts and swords out of branches and duct tape. He and his friends also loved to re-enact history in Axis & Allies and fight virtual enemies in video games like *Call of Duty*. Didn't most boys? But there were no Boy Scouts, peewee leagues or any organized activities for my independent-minded son then. Even the routine of school bored him, except when he was inspired by a real-to-him issue like why the Avro Arrow was cancelled, or raising funds for cancer research by shaving his head, long before it became popular.

Then, one night when he was 15, Nik and two buddies dropped into the local army cadet program—seduced, I think, by the opportunity to shoot real weapons. Ironically, his anti-war grandfather had introduced him to guns and target shooting when he was younger. Of the three friends, only Nik signed up; he already had the shaved head (or was it a mohawk then?). The parents of the other boys didn't approve, but my husband and I were more surprised than concerned, deciding that supervised marksmanship might be preferable to the mimicry in violent video games. And I didn't believe that a boy who usually railed against structure and group-think would last long. In generations past, in some schools, cadet classes had been compulsory; however, these days parents often enrol their sons and daughters in cadets for the rare discipline the program fosters, not as an introduction to army service.

Yet every week, as he polished his boots and ironed his uniform, Nik raved about the "useful" things that school wasn't teaching him, such as map reading, wilderness survival and leadership. He thrived in the fraternity and camaraderie that many of his peers found more digestible in team sports. I watched, amazed at how the merit system, command hierarchy and drill discipline all made sense to him. Sending me and his equally uninitiated Facebook friends a drill video, he commented, "You will see what kind of mental discipline it must take to be able to do this, as well as the physical coordination and teamwork, not to mention the choreographic finesse that went into the planning." Never one to train or exert himself unnecessarily, he would now run until he puked on testing day, just to meet the gold standard.

On Remembrance Day 2006, I couldn't help but be impressed as my son solemnly stood guard for hours at the local cenotaph, as oblivious to the minus-30-degree temperatures as the beret-clad vets he was honouring. But after a couple of months in Vernon, BC, at the Army Cadet Training Centre with some other cadets who treated the experience more as the summer camp it was, he announced he was ready for the real thing. I remember hoping he'd learn how to make his bed properly; was the army instead going to be his twisted version of teenage rebellion?

As Nik filled out the application for the Armed Forces and collected glowing references, I stifled my reservations but did my own research. It wasn't surprising that the Armed Forces would want him. I learned that it could sometimes be a challenge to find candidates from comfortable, educated urban Canada (in contrast to the draft of the Second World War, or the long lines of applicants in the First World War, trying to avoid the mines, factories or hunger of being unemployed). Nik easily met their minimum requirements of age (16), education (Grade 10) and fitness (which includes being able to perform 19 sit-ups and 19 push-ups). To my relief—because he still had high school to finish—his choice was the part-time reserve force, not the full-time regular force. And he still needed a parent's signature for his application because he was not yet 18.

During the First World War, mothers could apparently approve their sons' applications or have them "stamped" LOB (Left Out of Battle) for any number of reasons, such as age, but as with cadets and the tattoo, I wasn't about to withhold my permission even if I believed I'd earned *some* input. Certainly others thought I should (at least, those who didn't try to buy him a drink). "Are you going to let him?" shocked friends and family asked. Some were anti-war in principle or opposed to Canadian involvement in Afghanistan. Some confused Iraq and Afghanistan and the US military with the Canadian Forces. Still others didn't understand the differences between the regular Forces and the reserves. Even when I clarified that he'd have to volunteer for any assignment, many still assumed "our Nik" would be shipped off to Afghanistan automatically and were probably already anticipating consoling me at a funeral. His paternal grandfather, a refugee from war-scarred Europe, fruitlessly reminded us, "They use real bullets over there!"

I had attended an 18-year-old's funeral that summer. His mother had been a neighbour and our kids had gone to school together; her seat at the front of the hall could have been filled by any of the mothers there. A good kid and a talented extreme mountain biker and skier, her son died doing something much more mundane in the company of other testosterone-fuelled teenage boys who are inclined to feel invincible. Although my son was younger, and thus far a risk taker in less physical ways, I couldn't help but see the funeral as an omen.

Being male is apparently the single largest risk factor for early death. The pattern of high-risk behaviour begins in adolescence and peaks during the early twenties then declines. Young men are particularly susceptible to reckless driving and crashes, and dying in the military after volunteering for it. And at my son's age, most adolescents are still in that crucial phase of establishing their identity and searching for role models. The warrior archetype must seem especially appealing: the US army recognizes that half of their army enlists before age 20, when they're enthusiastic, fit and, maybe, naive. No wonder the recruitment ads of our own Armed Forces feature the adventure and excitement of jumping out of airplanes.

The next funeral I found myself attending was for a soldier killed in Afghanistan, Canada's 71st death, Corporal Nathan Hornburg, a member of King's Own Calgary Regiment (KOCR). The KOCR cadet troop, of which Nik was a member, attended together. Perhaps because Nik had begun his military application process by that time, I felt drawn to attend as well. From separate vantage points, Nik and I witnessed the impressive parade of soldiers slow-marching to the beat of the military band's funeral dirge. In the eulogies and tributes that followed, Nathan seemed a model citizen and son. Val Fortney from the *Calgary Herald* wrote:

> Like so many modern-day soldiers, the 24-year-old reservist was an educated young man, born into a life of comfort, security and opportunity. His decision to serve Canada in Afghanistan was no flight of fancy, nor was it a case of blindly following his superiors.

I couldn't help but identify with Nathan's mother, who confirmed, "he had all these choices and this is what he chose; it sort of boggles our minds," in a Remembrance Day speech only six weeks after the funeral. She spoke of standing behind her son without what she called "worry vibes." Sharing her stoic outlook and message—"Find what you would die for, and live for it"—probably made her the real hero to my son, who I observed listening as stiff-shouldered as his soldier brethren to romantic words of honour, duty, courage.

After the funeral, Nik seemed unusually quiet on the drive home together, but he made a point of reading aloud the verse on the funeral pamphlet: "Children are a sacred trust we've been only loaned for a short time. You are the bows from which your children as living arrows are sent forth." I recalled reading that same passage from Kahil Gibran in my own youth. Now I was reading the words of anthropologist David Gilmore, who explained that sacrifice and service to others might be a defining characteristic of manhood, a crucial and universal aspect of being a "real man." Apparently, the military model offers an acceptable if risky route to accelerated manhood: the Forces were becoming more relevant, attracting more volunteers than ever before, in spite of, or maybe because of, the caskets coming home from Afghanistan. And even with the presence of women, the army is still undeniably macho—most appealing when there's a war on. A mission promises action, trumping any simulations exercises.

Less than a month after Nathan's funeral, my soldier-wannabe turned up late for the first of his army interviews. I may have signed the form and lent him my car, but I wasn't going to drive him there. I let him find his way to the city alone, to a place he hadn't been to before, and where I knew there was little available parking. However, I may have also inadvertently helped Nik prepare for his interview, drilling him on why he wanted to join, what he could contribute, how it would fit with his other or future plans. I wanted to know, too. He'd already ruled out commissioned officer training and military college, preferring to be a "real soldier," get his hands dirty and work his way up. But he made the reluctant concession to apply to his hometown university, which would allow him to combine school with soldiering in his chosen regiment. He thought he might teach social studies or run for public office someday—but "after some life experience," he stressed.

With a sense of dread mixed with pride in his confidence and determination, I wished for a support network myself to help me work through the contradictory feelings I had around the military creed. It dawned on me that one such group did exist: the Military Family Resource Centre. It would be there for me when and if Nik became an official member of the military family, but how objective would it or could it be? In the meantime, a friend referred me to a book, *Soldier's Heart*, written by someone who had faced similar qualms—a civilian

English professor at West Point, Professor Elizabeth Samet. Sending soldiers off to an ill-considered early death was no abstract concept to her. She insisted her soldier students read the line in Horace's ode "*Dulce et decorum est pro patria mori*" and discuss whether it really was a great honour to fight and die for your country. Like me, she felt the need to challenge the accepted truths and the multiple contradictions of the military world in which she was a neophyte. But she also came to the conclusion that to find your place in the world as an adult is no easy task, and having a supportive community might be one of those good antidotes to all the hardships.

While Nik waited the best part of a year for the army bureaucracy to deal with his misdiagnosed asthma and other obstacles, he kept busy with weight training, rugby, Model United Nations and an expanding social life. I hoped his diversifying civilian life would give him perspective and new choices. Perhaps there would be no battle, after all, on any front?

Then the day came when he received his acceptance to his regimental family. It was the same day as his marks arrived for the provincial exams that would secure his academic future. Whooping, he left the marks letter unopened and rushed off to turn in his cadet uniform at the Legion. Nik couldn't wait to share what he called the "most important news of my life" with his cadet officer instructors— even though they had encouraged him to stay in school and in cadets until he aged out at 19. They'd advised him instead to take advantage of international cadet exchanges and paratrooper courses for which he had qualified through his performance on national cadet exams. "Not a chance," Nik responded; he was delighted to let other deserving cadets take his place. The real world was calling.

But I still had to wonder if he would have the right stuff for BMQ (Basic Military Qualification)—the standard test of endurance, a training camp that lasted a whole summer to weed out the uncommitted and physically or emotionally unfit. His habit of questioning anything illogical never seemed to work well in the Hollywood version of boot camp, such as in *Full Metal Jacket*, which we had once watched together. He hated my teasingly referring to it as "camp"—to him, it was the real deal, the adult world where few were younger than him. He trained to walk, talk and act like a soldier from the crack of dawn until well after dark through mind-numbing drills, lectures and the standard deprivations of a military life. But on the rare occasions when he could and did call home, Nik tried to assure me he was aware that the army teaches a soldier to submit his will to authority through inconsequential things such as haircuts and middle-of-the-night fire "pickets" just so he could be trusted to respond appropriately under more serious conditions. What the hell was a fire picket, I wanted to know? Still on alert for brainwashing, I delved further into military psychology. The powerful Pavlovian conditioning he was experiencing apparently ensures the body continues even when the mind shuts down. Good for a battlefield situation, no doubt, but how would it work on the home front, I wondered?

Sacrificing individual personal welfare for the good of the team was another concept familiar to cadets such as Nik, but he told me it was often a shock to some of the other young (and even older) people who were also "trying out" the army that summer. Everything they did had to be done as a unit, their performance dependant on helping each other while inculcating the infamous esprit de corps that was supposed to serve to unite them and disconnect them from the rest of the non-soldier world—a place Nik called "civvy street," after he made it through the summer with high ratings and invaluable self-awareness. His tattoo was to be his reward, he told me proudly before he left the base to come home. My consolation prize? He asked my opinion on the designs he was considering.

The army's habits, rough slang, black humour and acronyms that Nik brought home along with his tattoo made up an unfamiliar language that required constant translation. Sometimes he humoured me; sometimes he preferred to guard it from potential misinterpretation or the disrespect of outsiders. "You can't really understand," I began to hear again and again, though he rarely spoke unkindly, in the style of the typical teenager he had never been. Ever since he'd learned to talk, he'd explained things to me and anyone who would listen in great detail. Perhaps he just didn't understand it well enough himself to explain the new culture and life that was as elusive and alien to me as the young man he'd recently become. When I referred to documentaries or books we'd shared or I'd scoured for insight—*Fifteen Days, On Combat, Truth Duty Valour*—I heard, "You won't learn what I know from books or videos." An unwelcome voyeur, now I was not only confused and anxious to be enlightened, I was often shut out.

The message, however, was becoming clearer. It wasn't so much the military but the transformation of boy to man that I wasn't getting or accepting. Even if he was equally surprised by his son's developing soldier persona, his father could relate better to Nik's desire to do something more meaningful than sitting passively in a lecture hall of 300. I, on the other hand, had hoped Nik would take more time to bridge his active and contemplative selves. I'd glimpsed this when one day he quoted Clausewitz's *On War*, the classic military philosophical text, which affirmed his own belief that "war is merely an extension of politics." But Nik was applying his intellect and strong work ethic to the army, not his university courses. He didn't hide from us the fact he was spending more time at the armoury and on field exercises than on campus his freshman year, saying he didn't feel he was letting anyone down if he didn't get up early to study. Even the appeal of his favourite video game, *Call of Duty*, had diminished in favour of the real thing.

Then came April Fool's Day 2009: the irony occurred to me only later. I remember trying not to choke on my herbal tea when Nik came in the door from one of his routine reservist Wednesday nights to say, "My name's on the list, Mum." In this most casual manner, he'd announced that his commitment to his part-time job and hobby was no joking matter. Having formally volunteered for Afghanistan, he'd been selected to accompany the next "task force," he said, which would put him in theatre the following spring. Unlike with his decision to join cadets, I didn't know how to react—except with questions. I needed to know what a task force was and how it proposed to use my teenaged son.

The usual option for rookie reservists like him is one of the less exciting jobs, such as gate security or chauffeuring visiting VIPs, safely behind the wire on the heavily secured base. But in the later days of Canada's commitment, the reservists, who made up as much as a third of missions, were being asked and trained to do more as the army battled burnout and heavy troop rotations. My trooper was glad: he was planning to put his body where his head already was and started a year of full-time preparation immediately after his university semester ended. Nik's sergeant had recommended him for specialty training on the armoured recovery tank: driving *outside* the wire. Nathan Hornburg's job.

I thought my son was too young to write his will—just one of the many things he had to take care of before he deployed. However, I discovered that more than 40 per cent of reservists are under 25: they are the most enthusiastic when they join up, and according to the experts, the natural flow of the army ensures the old teach the young and the young inspire the old. I could only hope this balanced their lack of experience in combat and softened war's corrosive effects. PTSD was no longer just a military acronym.

One Sunday night that spring, I was still dwelling on mental health and wills when Nik returned from another weekend field exercise exhausted but clearly exhilarated about finally practising what he had signed up to do—reconnaissance. Reconstructing the training exercise in diagrams so I'd understand, he told me that not having been seen and not having to shoot his weapon were the measures of his unit's success. Perhaps he was just trying to appease me in an odd sort of role reversal, so I teased him about playing soldier just like when he was a kid, and for once he did not take offence. He and I knew it wouldn't be fun and games where he was going. And even though I wished he wasn't in such a hurry to join the adult world, I had to admit he was probably more ready than most teens.

No matter what I thought or felt, Afghanistan was calling my son. In the metaphor he identified with from *On Combat* by Lt. Col. Grossman, the bible for psychological preparation for battle that we both devoured after I tracked it down online for him, Nik told me he sees himself as the warrior/sheepdog. Sheepdogs are the self-appointed protectors of the world of good sheep, who like to pretend the bad wolf will never come. "Like sheepdogs, warriors deliberately go into harm's way at great risk; they believe in something greater than themselves."

Playing even a small role has always been important to this young citizen-soldier as he willingly and consciously takes on adult responsibilities in a complex world. He didn't see himself as expendable fodder, and I wanted to believe he was not just "ardent for some desperate glory," as the war poet Wilfrid Owen once warned, but truly standing up for what he believes in.

I knew I had to surrender—let him go, accepting that throughout history, the relationships between mothers, sons and battlefields have never been easy. This is the battle he chose and won; all I could do was to support him and stifle my worry vibes.

Epilogue: One of the lucky ones, Nik returned home unscathed. His mother, however, is still shaking.

EMBED

(An excerpt from *The Art of Witness: A Poet's Road to Afghanistan*)

S.M. Steele

He's Come Home Again

Sweet sweet, clean prairie Spring, he's come home again;
moon-dust Afghanistan sponged from his body, his face,
a fine Chinook cleansed him with hard rain,
prairie rain pushing silver-blue, the flax open again,
tiny blades of grass, the fast fox red feathering
the new-born stalks. Brown hawks circle, return
conquer earth as he patrolled sand
despair—ricochet, near miss, glanced bullet
shot heat: KAF's putrid, poison air.

Then left right left into the wired spider trap
Afghan winter; he tried so hard to inhale, breathe,

hang on to Spring. Oh now comes the petaling,
now, comes the shattering—season forever emptying.

Now comes the never shall be.

In memory of Cpl. Darren James Fitzpatrick, wounded March 6, 2010, Afghanistan, died March 20, 2010, Edmonton, age 21.

• • •

Embedded on neither the front nor the home front, I was, I am, a witness. Of the tribe of travellers, the civilian war artist. Observer. Listener. Recorder. Maker. Imaginer. Dreamer. I belong to no one. I belong to everyone. Sense, reorder, record, remake war, in my own image, my imagining. I went into war naive, searching for the unknowable, the elusive, something I thought might be called truth.

Embedded as an artist, witness, with a battalion heading for war, curiously I became embedded on neither the front nor the home front, that is, until I fell in love. Knew love, as perhaps only one who knows the intimacy of war might.

Passionately.

• • •

I met L in a freezing cold tent at Shilo, where he was setting up a Command Post (CP) for a newly mustered rifle company to deploy to Afghanistan a year later. We didn't notice each other; we were married to others and had no reason to look at each other except with fear (mine, because he was fierce) and disdain (his, because he hated lazy poets, but at least he was honest about it). We didn't track each other, as we both were focused, very focused on one thing and one thing only—Afghanistan.

It was my first Exercise (Ex) away from my cozy cottage on the west coast of Canada—a home with a husband, a child, two dogs, a cat, a half an acre of wild garden filled with roses, lavender, lilacs and Italian honeybees. At the invitation of the commanding officer, I flew out to Manitoba to be embedded with a battalion on their road to war, and ended up sleeping on a hard army cot amongst the men from Administration Company (Admin Coy) when I wasn't bouncing around in the gunner's turret of a Light Armoured Vehicle (LAV) or feeling sick to my stomach from the thunder percussion on the Carl Gustav (recoilless rifle) range.

At the time I didn't know the difference between a sergeant, a sergeant major and a major. The road to war in army camps and in Afghanistan was a steep learning curve for a civilian poet, an official war artist chosen to record the experience of war from a Canadian perspective. The diesel, hard edge of steel, sleep deprivation, the smell of canvas, those God-forsaken Canadian Forces' menopausal heaters that suffocate with heat, then shut down and leave one freezing, lack of privacy, illness, constant sound, constant readiness, strange food, constant stimulation, swagger, fear, suicide, death, away from all that was familiar, my quiet, leafy home with the wood stove by the ocean, and my family life. But I threw myself into it. Two years later, after he came home from Afghanistan, L said to me, "You know PL (Poet Laureate), in the 24 years I've been in the army, I never saw anyone put themselves through so much for their work." This from a former Airborne.

What I didn't know then, that autumn day in Shilo as I embedded with the troops, was that once I left home for war in 2008, I would never be able to fully return home again. The question I ask myself repeatedly though, is did I leave home, or did my home leave me? Maybe I'll never know.

War is the making or the breaking of us. I have seen greatness and the lowest through war. It is the frying pan that heats and brings out the very best, the tastiest in those we love—unconditionally, as in the case of my mother and daughter who had so much to lose should I die, yet both of whom urged me to "finish what you set out to do" when I faced unbearable personal hardship. But war can burn, singe, asphyxiate with choking smoke and can bring out the very worst, the tasteless, the vile, with poison of insecurity, jealousy, abandonment, betrayal and hatred.

And one never knows who will step up, who is capable of stepping up, or who will lose nerve and faith. Senior officers and NCOs (Non-Commissioned Officers) told me they never knew who would be the good soldier until the test of combat, and often it was the one least expected to excel. The same might apply to the home front; one never knows who will be dependable until the test of war. And faithlessness, that rusty blade of war, that sad intemperate thing, that cliché, wears many, many guises: criticism, sexual, weakness, lack of character, betrayal.

Nothing is worse for a person heading into the danger zone than to have the underpinnings of home withdrawn. *Nothing.* I know a soldier who was dumped via satellite phone the day after he was injured in an IED explosion and had lost a beloved comrade. He called home from his hospital bed and his fiancé hung up on him. Another was dropped by a fiancé just before he left for Afghanistan (he was killed on his tour); another was thrown out of the house days after returning home.

Some partners didn't wait until deployment but informed partners after an Ex, "We're done." Yet overwhelmingly, most on the home front kept the faith, carried on with fortitude, selflessness.

What the home front may find difficult, especially in the year leading up to war, during deployment and then immediately afterwards, is that when one faces death together with others, some alchemy happens between those on the same road. Heading for war, an indescribable bond with others on the same trajectory occurs, and a self-centredness of self-preservation kicks in, which might be perceived by loved ones as egoism or withdrawal. The constant song in someone's head who is going into war is, "Will I? Will I? Will I be dead this time next year?" The home front, meanwhile, hears a different tune, "Will he, will she? Be dead this time next year?"

The bond is survival. Even for war artists. No matter how hard I tried to be detached from soldiers, always called them by their ranks, never by first names, never socialized with them . . . it was impossible not to feel something for these human beings that were purposefully, as was I, putting themselves into serious danger. And that the grease of the wheel that binds those heading into danger is humour, a most endearing of human traits (the only time I didn't hear laughter was outside the wire in Afghanistan, the night before a big operation, and all was silent). Their humour is sarcastic, politically incorrect, pranks, jokes, and filled with "in" language (e.g., their astonishingly humorous and imaginative variations on the word "cock," such as "über-cock," meaning something that is a real waste of time or designed to annoy— "Go fill those sandbags, move them over there, then move them back and empty them" is a classic example of an über-cock exercise). The truth is, ask most soldiers who they fight for and while the party line might be for one's country, in reality, it is for each other—the ones who have suffered, laughed, conquered fear together.

The sense of "apartness" from the home front is also a survival technique for someone heading into a war zone—it's not wise to bring the preparations for war, or war itself, into the home. It's not uncommon for a soldier to keep souvenirs from tours in a box and not have anything in the house on display, except maybe a beautiful Persian carpet, a few Pashmina shawls or the standard-issue Dubai pearls they bring their mothers and daughters, sisters and wives. Many soldiers put a mental Hesco around their work and/or home life. This helps them separate their worlds, their two homes.

Sometimes the home front recognizes this, accepts there is a "no go" part of their loved one's life. The faithful trust that though the combatant, the loved one, *must* go, must leave and focus on comrades, mission and their calling—this is imperative, this is who they *are*— they will, with patience, love, kindness and compassion, *Insha'Allah*, God willing, return home, not just whole, but even better than before.

I wrote this before I left for Afghanistan:

Letter Before I Leave #1
forgive me. falling in love with this. obsessed. eating, drinking, sleeping with war. my possessions meaningless. that I could forget coziness. winter fire. warm food. lit candles. the duvet. my thoughts half a world away. on someone else's hardship. someone else's dismay. homes shattered. forgive me. the ice of Ex. buried us. a year of my life rolled across prairie like tumbleweed. I forgot to need. forgive me. falling in love with all of this. believing that just maybe. I could make a difference. with words. alone.

believing you could wait, be patient. keep coziness. winter fire. warm food. lit candles. the duvet. for me. 'til I came home. if only you could. believe. I would return. forgive me.

I witnessed the battalion, soldiers, alive on Ex. I witnessed them outside the wire in the theatre of war. I was also to witness them dead. A funeral. A repatriation. I stood on the tarmac alongside the mother, the father, the brother, of a lovely boy I knew, a boy with whom I shared homemade chocolate cookies—cookies sent to me by a kind person who baked them for me so that I was to have a taste of home away from home. I met soldiers' parents, their girlfriends, their children, their next-of-kin. A father phoned me every night for one winter. He cried every night that long winter until his boy was home.

• • •

After watching the battalion for a year, I flew outside the wire in November 2009. The 35-minute Chinook ride from Kandahar Airfield (KAF) in southern Afghanistan to that gorgeous, lethal mud-brick village out in Dand where the rifle company I knew best had set up its Headquarters (HQ), its new home. That flight was the strangest, most exciting commute to work in my life.

The flight, a fast and low zigzag over the Arghandab River, across the red Rajistan desert that claws into Afghanistan from Pakistan, flew over the infamous Ring Road, where a truck and an RPG (Rocket-Propelled Grenade) could do real damage. Once aloft I lost all fear, put faith in God's hands ("there are no atheists in the trenches"). I peered out of the little window behind me and saw wild camels scramble over the desert, the *Kuchi* nomads encamped in round black tents by the river, their goats and sheep penned, their women kneeling by the water beating laundry, smoke coming from their cooking fires. As we banked sharply, I saw, only a few hundred metres beneath us, compounds with multiple wives and children sitting on door stoops, while the husband/father looked up at us—their veils, their loose clothing flapped from the drafts of our Chinook's rotors. I could peer into their homes and see how entire lives could be lived within four mud-bricked walls.

We landed in a dust storm outside a little village in Dand District. I ran down the ramp, removed my helmet, ballistics, unwrapped my *shmawg*, and shook hands with the Officer Commanding (OC), Major, whose rifle company I'd been embedded with in Canada. As Major shook my hand, I felt something in my palm—a coin struck for the Afghan deployment and given only to members of the rifle company. "Welcome, Suzanne, you're one of the family now," Major said. "Get settled, the boys will set you up, then come back and we'll eat some of the lamb the Afghans slaughtered this morning for a *shura*." As I walked through the compound surrounding an abandoned Russian schoolhouse, I saw person after person I'd met and spent time with at Shilo, Suffield, Edmonton and Wainwright. I'd left home many times to be with them.

• • •

Diary Entry, October 2008
they call me Ma'am, drive me, deliver me, cinch my helmet
strap, my frag vest tight, escort me through prairie night, one
in front, one behind, C7s arc left C7s arc right, teach me turret
and gun, how to see like a hawk, boil my rations in a tin pot,
toast my toast with bayonet, share their p.b. and jam, swap
cheese spread for desiccated bread, listen to Metallica, rap,

Rage Against the Machine, Wake Up!, Slipknot, let me peruse their porn mags, offer me hand-rolled fags, show the bear claw worn around neck, tiger carved of jade, Mary medallion in vest, photo of eight-month-old son kept next to left breast, tell me how chere maman threatened to throw them down the stairs when they signed up, laugh and swagger and smoke and shout, keep me warm (curled mother wolf between them) after lights out when it's frigging cold and I've got no more layers to put on, let me ask a thousand questions, take a thousand notes, let me watch them sleep armoured up, their lashes angels', lips full, so young, a thousand million kisses yet to come, if all goes well in Afghanistan, the desert, the sand, the patrols, the reccies, the strong points, next year, if all goes well for them, should the boys come home again.

•••

With them I'd been hungry, bored, laughed, stood sentry, heard confessions, war stories, love stories. I even got sick with them. At Suffield I puked on live-fire and was hauled off in a Bison (ambulance), taken into Role 2 medical post where an overzealous medic injected Gravol into my skinny bicep with an infantryman-sized needle and infantryman technique that caused bruising for weeks, then was placed in an isolation tent and forgotten for 24 hours. "You're one of us for sure now, Ma'am," said Cpl., one of the Regimental Quartermaster's (RQ) men, as he delivered a care package and a heater to my freezing pup tent, "Everybody has to get sick and forgotten on Ex. at least once in a career!" The Company Quartermaster (CQ) and RQ's people were always very, very good to me.

I shared a room outside the wire with four men—two enlisted, an intelligence officer who nervously asked, "Who is she? Is she okay?" ("She's okay," the young soldiers replied) and a "cultural advisor," a bearded Afghan Canadian. I only knew two of my roommates' real names. In the corner, leaning against the wall, were two AK-47s, and two M-6s. The roof above my cot had just been replaced after a mortar attack a few weeks earlier. "Don't worry, mortars are like lightning; they never strike the same place twice," they all reassured me. I wasn't.

The home away from home in Afghanistan was as comfortable as possible given that any second we could be mortared, have to grab kit, weapons, pack and run into our LAVs within minutes. Beside the shower tent there was a ripped leather sofa—the "lounge." There was a snack tent filled with chips, nuts, sugary cereal, bread and cheese for grilled cheese sandwiches (which cooks tell me the soldiers prefer to prime rib, as they remind them of home). There was instant hot chocolate, coffee and the ubiquitous, much loved "gay" (ya, they know it's un-PC) Irish Cream coffee creamers. There was a foosball table that young Afghan National Army (ANA) soldiers gravitated toward, and a slow drip of wireless for laptops upon which the boys played games, checked Facebook and watched the same videos over and over again.

One night I helped the senior NCOs cook dinner. I liked to keep busy on Ex. and overseas, and I found that helping out was a good way to see how the soldiers were doing. That night under the violet, starry Afghan sky, we barbecued chicken, made a big pot of mashed potatoes, boiled peas, served apple pie. At dusk 150 hungry guests rolled into the compound in their dusty LAVs and Coyotes. "The hotel is full tonight," said Major as we scrambled to feed extra mouths. I rifled through the medics' freezer for hamburger pucks and hot dogs. We cooked everything in sight and served the exhausted boys. I slapped spuds on their plates, winked at the youngest ones, looked them in the eye, asked, "How's it going?" But I could see how it was going. They were exhausted, and this was their first big Op into real war. They were excited and frightened. Some were homesick. This was no video game or war game at Wainwright. Nobody was dead. Yet.

I never slept the whole time I was there. Not in KAF, waiting for rocket attack sirens to go off, nor in the Russian schoolhouse where I felt most at home with the men and women I knew best. I lay awake and thought about L. He slept in the room next to ours, separated by three feet of stone wall construction. We'd met when our home fronts were as they should be—intact—but mine imploded just before I was to go to Afghanistan, I didn't see it coming, while his waited until he arrived home from the war, exhausted and grieving the loss of his men. But that was months ahead. He had no clue what was coming as he slept and worked in Afghanistan.

At night when I went to the toilet, a young soldier always had to accompany me. He carried a pistol. He longed to go on patrol outside the wire but was confined to the HQ because his mother was critically ill at home in Canada and someone was watching over him. He was angry and depressed. All he wanted was to get into the war—as if being in an HQ outside the wire wasn't enough.

The ANA's room on the other side of us had ruby-coloured carpets and soft lighting. AKs leaned against the wall and boots were lined neatly on the stair outside. They had their own cook, who made fresh *naan* and mutton and gorgeous-looking food. They ate on real dishes, drank tea from real glass cups unlike us, who ate off paper and plastic. The Afghans were curious about me and wondered why I didn't carry a weapon, only a pen. When they were told that I was a *sha'ir*, a poet, they understood. It wasn't strange to them, a poetry-loving culture, that a poet might fly to Afghanistan to spend time with the Canadian army.

I left the rifle company in late November, or rather, they left me as they headed out on their first big Op into the danger country. Before they left several asked me to contact their families when I was back in Canada. After I flew home to Canada I called mothers and fathers and girlfriends. I lied and lied and lied to them: I reassured them that their loved ones were in the *safest* part of Afghanistan and that they weren't taking any chances and that they were warm and comfortable and bored. I *didn't* lie when I told the families that the OC and Sgt. Major were not putting their people into any danger that they themselves wouldn't undertake—more than one soldier said they'd follow their OC and Sgt. Major anywhere. I told loved ones that their soldiers were doing what they felt called to do. And though I saw fear and discomfort and heard soldiers bitch (a soldier who doesn't bitch is a troubled soldier, or so I'm told), I saw fully engaged people who wanted to be there.

That winter, after I came home from Afghanistan to a quiet and often empty house, was so damned long, so cold, so damned hard. I came home to Canada but couldn't really come home. This is hard for the home front to understand.

The rifle company lost five men overseas. I knew two others from the PRT (Provincial Reconstruction Team) who were killed and I'd been in the presence of all of the dozen from the battle group who were killed that year. Some soldiers came home to joy, others to trouble. In 18 months since coming home there have been marriages and babies, divorces and suicides. The IED of PTSD simmered in some, flashed hot in others.

L came home to a shitshow. But in the end, miraculously, because neither of us ever imagined it, we found each other again after a memorial service for the fallen. We spent the first Remembrance Day after war together, and then a month later honoured the first anniversary of his officer's death by going snowshoeing in the wilderness. In a grove on the frozen shore of Elk Island with only a single wolf for company, we made a little nest with our coats; drank espresso made on our camp stove; ate Brie, a baguette, black chocolate and grapes; and spilled single malt for the lost soldier. A single raven flew above us. My man laughed, said, "My friend, I never imagined you as a raven. Thanks for showing me you're okay." We drove back to the city, took each other tenderly/fiercely to our new, warm bed, as only lovers who have been through a war together can.

That winter, that lovely, lovely winter of 2010–11, after Afghanistan, we brought each other home.

Lazarus (12)
thank you. thank you
you wrote. exquisite. cursive. rows on rows. your handwriting
on an A.Y. Jackson note
a week after you left my west coast. little beauty.
each S. each O. your kisses like snowshoes. snowshoes. snow-
    flakes. ice.
lips. cool white tracers along my naked back. I let you in.
I let you in.
blue tattoos. orange lightning bolt. PATRICIA zzzzzappp!
Airborne. Regimental crown.
I want to love again. I want to love again. you mouth these words
beneath the surface of your winter ice. *love. again.*
and L, you did.

You took my axe. split winter wood for my winter stove
until the axe of four o'clock split your jaw.
and the Afghan axe which split your skull wedged in.
and the faithless's axe split your breastbone.
your breastbone axed. and the axe axed. you in
two

so I drew you a bath. took you to bed. late afternoon.
again. and again.

Leaves. crisp. sweet. coastal winter. curling crisp, maple leaves.
soft. soft. you
could smell them again. you laughed. after you awoke.
with you I taste. Christ, with you I breathe. again.

you left my warm blankets, sheets, at 5 AM. dressed in the dark
so as not to waken me. laced up your boots. zipped, buttoned
    temperates.
greens.
boots. shiny. black. polished. perfection. sheen.

later, you txted me from the field,
with you I feel content, satisfied
more so than in years and years
thank you baby
thank you.

TERRIBLY BEAUTIFUL:
REMEMBRANCE AND REMEMBERING

Kari Strutt

The air was absolutely still the day I came undone with war.

It was November 11, 1981, on a flat piece of lawn at the base of the monument at Vimy Ridge. I had a snare drum slung from my shoulder and balanced against my thigh. Every piece of my uniform was properly pressed and my boots gleamed like no others in the parade.

It was clear that day, and cold. The bright grass hardened into green spines that snapped under our feet. The lead trumpet, a pimple-faced man named Matt, coaxed the Last Post from the hard throat of his frozen instrument.

As he sounded the Post's last note, the children from Arras came running, each child clutching a single red rose and racing, striding to be the first to lay the rose at the foot of the mammoth stone woman with the broken heart.

They could not wait for Matt to finish. His final note still sounding, the children erupted, their hot breath streaming behind, small clouds holding firm on the still air, contrails, frail evidence of life moving.

I tried to remember what I was supposed to remember, but the children filled my head. As the fog of their breathing cleared, I wept instead.

• • •

Remembrance Days are now divided into those that occurred before I visited Vimy Ridge and those that came after.

Before Vimy, during the moment of silence, I generally tried to fill that quiet time with thoughts of gratitude. I was only marginally successful.

My thoughts sometimes drifted to what everyone around me might be thinking. I was certain there was at least one person compiling a grocery list. Another had a runny nose and was trying not to sniff. Someone was regretful he didn't pee before the speeches began.

• • •

The war I experienced in my early years was served Cold.

Growing up, the television was forbidden during the main course, but an appetizer or dessert of evening news brought the fighting to the dinner table almost every day.

The first war I witnessed was Vietnam. Television allowed us to watch our men shooting their men. I often watched the neighbourhood boys, holding sticks that looked like guns, rolling over snowbanks and diving behind cars—staccato shooting noises popping through smiling lips. The television war was clearly different. There were no smiles; I could tell a live body from a dead one—even in black and white.

When I asked my dad if he could get drafted all the way from Canada, I wanted him to say no. Instead he laughed and said, "If it gets so bad that the army needs guys as old as me, we're in real trouble." I know he was trying to be funny, but when children bring up such topics, they are usually quite serious. He could have told me it was not our war. He could have told me they only called boys to that war.

Later that year, 1969, I watched the first troop withdrawal from Vietnam. I was positively joyous because I was certain that from now on, all the daddies would be with their little girls. I said very complimentary things to God that night.

It took many more years before I understood that those men from Vietnam, or others who looked exactly like them, would eventually be shipped to another place, another battlefield. It took decades to realize that when we forget to remember, it usually ends badly for someone.

• • •

In Grade 6, my teacher rolled a television into the classroom. We were going to witness history. Live.

We watched in wonder as the Canadian hockey team did what no government seemed capable of. A shot from close range, a quick rebound, and suddenly, it was over . . .

Paul Henderson won the Cold War.

I am quite certain that every Canadian alive that day remembers that goal.

We didn't have to be afraid of the Russians anymore. We had beaten them. In fact, I kind of felt sorry for them, especially Valeri Kharlamov. I was 12 years old and certain we were not meant to hate anyone that handsome.

. . .

In the summer of Grade 12, I read the description of the Naval Reserve summer employment program and thought it sounded like day camp for big kids. There would be morning runs, swimming, a wilderness survival trip, marching, tae kwon do, boating and enough money to pay for tuition in the fall.

We were a tribe, life was a grand adventure, and nothing bad would befall us. We had no quarrel with any nation or political philosophy. We were having fun. We were young and fit and fully engaged in the process of creating our good old days. (It occurs to me now that this attitude might be the dominant prerequisite for the initiation of mass armed conflict.)

It turned out I was a model Wren, best in class. I still have the trophy.

By the end of that summer I had won a new group of friends. Few of my high school friends went on to university, but all my naval friends were headed that way. We—the engineering students, the English majors, the computer science guys—traded our recruit epaulettes for those of Able Wrens and Seamen, and stayed on as reserves.

. . .

The military musician receives special treatment. It is the only trade in the Forces that exists to entertain or inspire, rather than defend. Oh sure, we all have to learn to fire weapons, but no one really expects the average flautist or French horn player to be particularly good at it.

On my first Remembrance Day as a military Naval Reserve musician, we performed at the ceremony at the Southern Jubilee Auditorium, and then the band was transported to Calgary's Number 1 Legion. We played a few old songs—"The White Cliffs of Dover," "Don't Sit under the Apple Tree," "The Way You Look Tonight"—and then there were some speeches. Eventually, the lights dimmed and occupants of the large room, mostly older gentlemen, were left with their own thoughts.

In less than 10 seconds, the first audible sob tore a hole in the quiet. Another followed quickly and the silence unravelled.

In this room were many men and women whose thoughts turned to remembered events.

I was grateful to have no such memories.

Oddly, when the moment of silence was past, the room quickly gave itself over to laughter and drinking and singing other old songs. Many stayed late into the night.

• • •

I took a semester away from university to travel through Europe with the band from CFB Gagetown. We played in Lahr and Baden, at NATO headquarters in Brussels and then at Vimy Ridge.

On the airplane flying to Germany, I finished reading *Nineteen Eighty-Four.* Oceania is at war with Eastasia. Oceania is at war with Eurasia.

Our big brother to the south was still at war with the Communists, stalking them from continent to continent, always one step behind. It was tempting to be amused. But it was 1981 and the new president, Reagan, was committed to finding every last one.

I couldn't remember where the most dangerous Communists were. I did remember that, buried deep in silos and strapped to the bellies of airplanes, there were 18,000 nuclear warheads available, should anyone care to use them.

Eighteen thousand. Enough megatonnage to pulverize every habitable space on the planet many times over.

I was only 20 and already I had serious concerns about political leadership. My cynicism solidified, like plaque on a tooth: protective, and at the same time destructive.

In 2011 those warheads seem forgotten. I wonder if they still exist. I hope someone is keeping track of them.

• • •

The motto of my naval base, HMCS Tecumseh, *In pace bellum para*, means "In peace, prepare for war."

But preparing for war while knee-deep in peace is a complicated affair.

It's easy to want to believe in peace. It's like believing in the tooth fairy, that gentle pixie who watches over our precious mouths and rewards our near-painless losses with small gifts. It's a myth that parents are content to foster in children.

But to believe in war, to believe so absolutely that you prepare for it . . . it's like inviting evil to creep under your pillow. This is the anti–tooth fairy, and she rips teeth out of your mouth while you sleep. She leaves you unable to chew, a mouth full of blood and nothing under your pillow but your own clenched fist.

In pace bellum para.

• • •

When I came home from my trip to Vimy Ridge, I quit the Naval

Reserve. I had to return to the military all of its "items of record"—the shirts, the cotton jacket and pants, the more formal wool blazer and trousers, the beret and bowler, the boots and shoes. The epaulettes. They did not want my socks. The process was streamlined. Surprisingly, no one tried to talk me into staying. Perhaps if I had taken a more useful trade . . .

The very next Remembrance Day I went shopping in a record store. I found a pin—almost two inches square with a black background, a white dove flying with a poppy firmly held in its beak. The pin asserts, "To Remember is to End All War."

As I pinned it to the pocket of my plaid shirt, it occurred to me that there is a difference between "remembering" and "acting like I remember." It's like the difference between being hungry and making a sandwich. Remembrance is not an excuse to ruminate; it is a call to action.

Thirty Remembrance Days later, I still have that pin.

• • •

On November 11, 1981, when I stood at Vimy Ridge watching the children run, flowers in hand, every one of them straining to win, I knew there would be another war—a real war, not a Cold one. A hot war, full of fire and burning. I knew it would not happen this year, or even the next, but it would happen.

As I stood in the shadow of a beautiful stone sculpture of Canada Bereft, I was certain that this new war would not be my war. It would take years for politics to shift, for the critical issue to arise, for the balance of power to weight itself to one side, for diplomacy to fail and the gauntlet to be tossed. By then I would be too old to fight . . . too old to die.

But the beautiful children that streamed past me . . . the next war might be theirs.

I focused hard, finding a face among the faces, green eyes, a mole on a cheek and a perfect lip with one small scar.

I committed that small face to memory. *I will remember.*

I searched for another.

I will remember you, too, you with the glassy drizzle of clear mucous running from nose to lip. I will remember your hair, badly cut, and your cowlick, the colour of poplar bark.

I captured as many faces as I could. Perfect tiny faces. I remember them.

The man next to me was from Grimsby, Ontario. He was a very good drummer. He gently tapped my drum with his stick.

I cried because I wanted, desperately, to stop some terrible thing that had not yet begun to happen.

This was my first real act of remembrance.

• • •

I have a friend, Dianna. Her son is a current-day reservist. He volunteered for a tour of duty in Afghanistan. During the months he was away, Dianna changed in the most extraordinary way.

Her face got thin, the skin folded in on itself, deep parenthetical gouges started at each cheekbone and ended near her chin. More dramatically, the body fat that cradled her heart began to build upon itself, layer after layer, until Dianna looked pregnant.

It was as if she was growing that absent boy again—remembering him in a place where she could keep him safe, keep him whole, trying to forget where he actually was.

Nine months later that boy came home safe. Dianna's belly returned to normal size, but her smile never fully recovered.

I sometimes wonder, during those months when she lay awake at night, flayed by the relentless anxiety, if she wished she could forget him, undo him just long enough to get a good night's sleep.

• • •

Last Wednesday a young man in a red Corvette roared up behind me, tailgated for a moment, then swerved into the left lane and passed. I hate being tailgated.

I'm also one of those people who changes behind the wheel. I can't really explain it. I've said things inside my shell of steel that I would never utter with my feet on the ground. I have worked myself into a rage that frightens my daughter and worries my husband.

When I pulled up behind the boy, I noticed that his car had a veteran's licence plate.

I wanted to get out of the car and grab that boy by the ear. I wanted to slap him, twice, tell him that someone has put a lot of time and effort and love into him. Tell him he should be more careful, if not for himself, then for his mother.

I wanted to tell him that she worries about him—all the time . . . and he's obviously doing a lot of stuff that's not helping.

My hands cramped because I was gripping the wheel too hard, and I was quivering. Moments like this moment instruct me.

I must be aware that there is a warrior in me, too. I've learned this before, and it's quite likely I'll learn it again.

Anger, like fear, is forgetful.

. . .

There is something undeniably feminine about the grassy hillocks and hummocks that form part of the Vimy Ridge landscape. Made by bombs, they would once have been slick with mud and blood but now they are covered in an even blanket of soft grass. They bring to mind the swell of breasts and buttocks and rounded bellies. It looks like a fine spot to sleep out underneath the stars, play a game of bocce, rest back against a tree, sip a beer.

It's difficult, standing in the sunlight, to comprehend the world that exists below. Under the soft, sweet waves of green are dark tunnels.

The stone walls that form the tunnels at Vimy are soft. They yield easily to the blade of a knife. For the waiting soldiers, anxious and bored, those cave walls became a canvas. Over time, they became a gallery of sorts. Some of the knife work is expert, done in relief—a maple leaf or a regimental crest.

Generally the carving is a name and a date.

The names are all different, but each one says the same thing.

Remember me. I was here.

. . .

There will be more war yet, not because we don't remember, but because we remember with hearts that have returned to normal size. We remember the singing, but not the cries of anguish. We remember the heroism, but not the panic. We remember men marching in time, not crawling in the mud.

Somehow, in our remembering we always manage to make the last war a bit more beautiful, a little less terrible. We put it to music and sing along.

This Remembrance Day I will return to Vimy, this time with my husband and my young daughter. I will wear my black pin with the white dove holding the poppy.

"To Remember is to End All War."

I will observe the silence, but remember that war is not quiet.

And I will buy poppies because, for all our remembering, there is a new generation of veterans who have made possible this terribly beautiful life we live and they need our help.

And for that day, I will not simply remember. For that day I will be mindful of my anger, cognizant of my fear. I will remind myself that the veneer of civilization is thin, that my actions can serve as varnish, or sandpaper. I will be part of the solution.

I will remember.

PLAYING BALL: RANDOM NOTES FROM BEHIND THE FRONT LINES OF THE PAX AMERICANA

Chris Turner

I. *The Old Ball Game*

The kid at the plate hoisting the bat up onto his shoulder is named Elias Kawar, and he's 14 years old and baby-fat pudgy, with smooth dark skin and a black jersey that says "Jordan," which is where he's from. Elias has got the whole routine down: he leans in, takes a couple of practice swings, then settles back, eyes fixed on the pitcher. Out on the mound is a lanky kid named Nir Pelter, also around 14, loose-limbed and wiry, his jersey light blue and almost shimmering in the brilliant late-morning sun, and it says "Israel." Nir's got his routine down, too: grabbing the rosin bag, tossing it aside, digging a rut in front of the rubber, then leaning out and squatting down, using his knee as a crutch, the ball hidden against his outfield-facing leg. They both lean in at once—pitcher and batter—and then Nir winds up with his front leg kicking high, and Elias' bat cocks back just a bit more, and the game's back on.

From the stands, the pitch is just a blur, but this stocky Jordanian kid sees it all the way in and turns it around with a sweet-spot crack. The ball soars, off like a rocket, and Nir and his teammates all look warily skyward. The left fielder doesn't even move; this one's gone and he knows it, 325 feet down the line and out. A home run. Elias knows this part too—he trots the bases slowly, cocky, like he knew it all along.

It's one of those classic Norman Rockwell scenes, pure Americana, everyone playing their part. As for mine, I'm up in the stands, busily scratching notes. I'm a staff reporter for the *Kaiserslautern American*, a weekly newspaper serving America's largest overseas military community, and I've picked this game over all the others on the 1994 European Little League Championship schedule because it's the only one being played by two teams whose home countries are, on this lovely day for baseball, officially at war.

So when Elias-the-Jordanian rounds third and Nir-the-Israeli starts over to the baseline to meet him, I can't help but catch my breath for a worried instant, anticipating the possible shattering of a delicate kind of dream. Because here are these kids, teenagers from Jordan and Israel, their teams perennial also-rans in the tournament, and they'd scheduled this exhibition game to mark a historic moment. Three days later—on July 25, 1994—King Hussein of Jordan and Israeli prime minister Yitzhak Rabin are going to meet in Washington and hammer out a peace treaty that will end the state of war that has existed between the two countries since 1967 (part of a violent conflict that dates 20 years further back). Just one year earlier, in the same tournament at this very site, the Jordanian team had refused—under palace order—to even share a field with the Israelis, forfeiting the game instead.

A "friendship game"—this is what the Israeli coach had called it. A fresh start. Such a beautiful idea. And like any really good baseball story, it's about way more than the game. It's a myth, an idea proscribed by basepaths and box scores about how much better a tidy ballpark of a world might be. Hence the little hitch in my breath, that slight tightening of gut. Because I'd been loving it: sitting in the stands, watching the kids work through baseball's timeless rituals as I listened to cheering in Arabic and infield chatter in Hebrew. I'd been thinking about the healing powers of the ole ball game, and thinking, too, that this has been the first taste this summer of the reason why I'd decided to pursue a career in journalism—to take a front-row seat at extraordinary moments like this, to witness some small slice of history.

Then, instead of being blown, the scene just gets better: Nir simply extends his arm in congratulations, and he and Elias slap hands and grin at each other. As if to say, "You know what? That was one hell of a dinger, and isn't it great to be playing baseball out here, in the warmth of a European summer? Doesn't that just beat the hell out of war?"

There it was: an instructive lesson in the wonders of the American way, played out on a baseball diamond on an American military base. Funny thing was there were almost no Americans involved.

II. How I Came to Be a Military Propagandist

I covered that Jordan and Israel baseball game, as I said, as a staff reporter for the *Kaiserslautern American*, a weekly morale-booster of a community newspaper run by the public affairs department of the 86th Air Wing of the United States Air Force (86 Wg/PA—the first but far from the last of my encounters that summer with the military's love of an acronym). The story ran more or less the way I've described it here, though newsier in tone of course. The headline was "Game Mirrors End to Old Animosity."

It was my favourite story from my summer as a US military propagandist, which was pretty much what you were when you worked for the *Kaiserslautern American*. The *KA*, as we referred to it, serves an entity called the Kaiserslautern Military Community (KMC), a grouping of two army installations, an army medical facility and a massive air base in southwestern Germany, which collectively make up the largest US military community outside the country's borders. The KMC is a central node in America's global military apparatus, the place from which Middle Eastern military actions are organized and to which the wounded in places like Bosnia and Iraq are brought for medical attention. It's a small city state airdropped into Germany from the American heartland.

The summer of 1994 was more or less the apex of America's sense of its lone-superpower status. It was a nation still basking in the glow of the fall of its Soviet archrivals, confident as ever in its central role in the global march of freedom. And the KMC was, in its way, the ultimate expression of the Pax Americana, the gun turret that delivered the castle's sense of self-satisfied security. And there I was, long-haired and earringed and two years into a history degree with a decidedly lefty slant, bringing the local news to these God-fearing American soldiers on the front lines.

It wasn't totally alien territory. My father was a fighter pilot in the Canadian Air Force, serving a term just then at a NATO desk job at Ramstein Air Base, the central node of the KMC. And I was a lifelong base brat, born and bred among uniforms and crisp salutes and supersonic fighter aircraft. My earliest understanding was that Santa Claus arrived dangling from a helicopter in a fighter helmet with a signal-orange Mae West wrapped around his neck, like he did at the Officers' Mess Christmas parties at CFB Chatham. I could identify all but the most obscure military aircraft by silhouette alone at 30,000 feet. As long as I live, I'll probably feel a warm, inviting sense of home whenever I hear that distinctive crackling rip of a fighter jet's engines tearing the sky apart high above me. On the surface, this was just another posting, another base.

In any case, the Canadian military guaranteed (and paid for) summer employment for the collegiate children of their overseas staff. From the *KA*'s point of view, I was free labour. Within weeks of arriving at the newspaper's office, I'd demonstrated enough basic skill to cover the sports beat, which meant Little League baseball and intramural golf tournaments and rewriting amateur press releases about the Kaiserslautern High School gymnastics team. And despite all the military uniforms in the office, it was surprisingly laid-back, a pretty cushy summer job.

More than that, though, it was a crash course in what makes Canada—and its military—so very different from their American cousins.

III. Northerners & Southerners, Part 1

I'm not sure whether the cultural gap between Canadians and Americans is bigger than we let on or if we're just more acutely aware, as Canadians, of every little difference. Anyway, it's something that I'd known in my bones since the age of seven, when my father was posted to St. Louis, Missouri, to consult with McDonnell Douglas Aero on the Canadian military's pilot training programs for the F-18s it had just bought.

After a year and a half in St. Louis and another couple of years in Denver, Colorado, I'd amassed a handful of American quirks (I still sometimes default to zee instead of zed, there's no eff sound in my pronunciation of "lieutenant," and I have an abiding love for baseball) and a vast catalogue of estrangements. The kids rising as one each morning to recite the Pledge of Allegiance. The boy across the aisle at lunch with his magical space-age "paper on paper" fruit snack. (This was the phrase I repeated over and over—*it was like paper on paper but one piece was fruit!*—as I tried to explain to my bewildered mother about the first Fruit Roll-Up I'd ever seen.) Baseball and football obsessions and the near-total irrelevance of hockey. My parents' dawning recognition that they were the only ones who socialized one-on-one with the black couple on the block. Real Southern barbeque, authentic Mexican food, Whatchamacallit chocolate bars. MTV and the Fourth of July.

Base brats are shape shifters by nature, raised in a culture that splinters apart and reorders itself across continents every few years. We watch for clues, pick up on patterns, note subtle differences between the ranking systems in social hierarchies as we switch from the cozy backwoods middle school in Cold Lake to the big urban high school in North Bay. Even still, there was nothing in Canadian military life quite like a full-sized American base.

My father had been part of the final closure of CFB Baden-Soellingen in the early 1990s, and when it was done he was transferred a few hours up the Autobahn to the USAF's Ramstein Air Base. The basic disposition of the two bases was a shorthand version of the greater incongruity. A significant chunk of the Canadian families—maybe even the majority—lived in rented homes in German villages near the base, and even the PMQs (Private Married Quarters) were outside the main gate. We ate dinner in *Gasthausen* and sampled the culinary delights on offer over the border in Alsace. The local hangout for older teens was a German-style café bar run by locals and frequented by new arrivals from the collapsed German Democratic Republic, who were eager to sample the Westernest vibe they could find. We snacked on *Döner* from the Imbiss and drank *Glühwein* as we Christmas shopped at *der Christkindlmarkt*. Even before my parents were posted to Germany, I was familiar with the distinctive European flair you'd find in fellow base brats recently returned from an overseas posting.

The population of the KMC, by comparison, skewed younger, poorer and disproportionately black, Latino and Southern. They mostly lived on the bases, spending US currency at the stores and fast-food joints on base (Burger King, Popeye's Chicken & Biscuits and Dunkin' Donuts among them), and there was a substantial security apparatus between all of it and anything German. There was some interaction, of course, but I doubt many of the American base brats went back to Texas or South Carolina with much of a European swing in their step.

The Americans, though, had as many lessons to teach me about foreign custom as the Germans did. American custom, I mean. One of the first and most strident was about barbeque. A couple weeks into my internship, 86 Wg/PA had a farewell cookout for one of the secretaries and it doubled as my baptism into the secular religion of barbeque.

As with the USAF in general, 86 Wg/PA teemed with Southerners. There was Eddie, the *KA* editor, who I believe was from Oklahoma. There was Major Turner (no relation), the chief of 86 Wg/PA, who was from the woods of Arkansas and couldn't wait to get back there. There was TSgt. Michelle R. Demers, who was a Texan. And a civilian reporter, Teresa Mattick, the wife of a Southern soldier, who was the kind of tall, blond, wide-grinned woman I thought was a Hollywood fiction. And there was Captain Law, young and gung-ho, with hair you could set a watch by and a penchant for Rottweilers and perfectly executed salutes. And of course there was The Colonel—I'm not sure if I ever knew his surname, he was simply The Colonel—who bore an uncanny resemblance to Hollywood actor Fred Thompson, famous for his multiple roles as the grizzled, drawling Southern authority figure.

I'd grown up confused and amused by the incongruity between Hollywood depictions of military life and my first-hand experience on Canadian air bases. There was little of the self-seriousness or hyper-formality I saw in the movies, few barked orders or ruler-straight lines of marching soldiers chanting out cadences, and my fighter pilot father, despite his charms, would never be mistaken for Tom Cruise. To my knowledge, he and his navigator had no super-cool *Top Gun* two-slap handshake, either, and no one I ever met at a CFB Cold Lake mess function had much in the way of a drawl. Who were these exotic animals in uniforms like my dad's? Turns out they were at 86 Wg/PA on any given workday.

There was a barbeque pit out behind the 86 Wg/PA building, a great wide low thing like a park fountain, full of charcoal instead of water. The first time I laid eyes on it, it was surrounded by Southerners deep in good-natured argument. There was a range of meats and sausages on the grill, but the conversation was mainly about the ribs— how long to cook them, when to flip them, when to baste, what spices, more charcoal or less. It was simultaneously easygoing and heated, in a distinctively Southern way—lots of *you don't know shits* and *whaddya think yer doins* and *y'all don't know the first goddamn thing about bar-beques.* Everyone agreed about certain basics, but God, freedom and the American way were in the details.

I knew barbeque mainly as a thing that occurred over roaring natural gas flames on PMQ patios—the lesser Canadian craft of grilling—and I fully conceded to the superior Southern art within a bite or two. They were the best damn ribs I'd ever had. The beer was cold and German and plentiful. And I learned, too, that there's a certain kind of explosive, boisterous laughter native to the American South—sudden and communal—that feels like a sort of benediction.

Once I'd experienced a few more of these 86 Wg/PA "training" days—a euphemism for knocking off at two o'clock or so on Friday afternoon, gathering in the conference room or out by the barbeque pit and indulging in a half-litre or two of the local pilsner ahead of the for-mal launch of the weekend—I was even ready to try my hand at casual Southern argument.

My first attempt was at an 86 Wg/PA training day not long after the fiftieth anniversary of D-Day. Captain Law—he of the Greenwich Observatory haircut—was regaling the room with stories of the anni-versary celebrations, explaining with palpable delight how some of the American Second World War veterans had booed President Bill Clinton, their draft-dodging commander-in-chief. Like a great many USAF soldiers of my acquaintance that summer, Captain Law hated Bill Clinton with an unguarded and intense zeal. He actually physi-cally winced when he first spied the official photo next to the president's way-to-go-boys spiel in the July Fourth edition of the *KA*.

Talk turned to the relative merits of the war that the young

Bill Clinton had skipped out on. There was universal agreement that the jeers of the D-Day vets were understandable, that men who had seen their friends die fighting for their country had earned the right to show Clinton as little respect as they wanted. And there was universal agreement, to varying degrees, that the Vietnam War was a necessary and just action, as ugly as it got.

My head filled with a thousand arguments I'd learned in my favourite history class at Queen's University (HIST 275: Conspiracy and Dissent in Twentieth Century America) the semester before—taught, not incidentally, by an American expat who'd left his homeland in disgust during the Vietnam War. I could explain the central fallacy of the domino theory with multiple references, detail the half-truths and outright fabrications of the Tonkin Gulf Incident in almost hourly detail, call instantly to mind the poetic cadences of Ho Chi Minh's Fourth of July appeals to the American people to honour the right of self-determination enshrined in their own Constitution. But I remained conspicuously silent a long while nevertheless, sipping my Warsteiner and chewing an inch and a half off my tongue, trying to figure out how to mimic that offhand Southern way of contradiction.

Finally, I underhand-pitched the suggestion that conscientious objection was far more common in 1968 than in 1941. This was met with grudging agreement from the rest of the room and a suspicious head tilt from Captain Law. Then Major Turner (no relation) changed the subject, and that was that.

IV. Even the French Eggs are Proud to Be American

At the Ramstein BX—the base exchange, the air base's supermarket—the eggs came in cartons with a special message printed on the underside of the lid. It read: THE ALSATIAN FARMERS PRODUCE EGGS GRATEFULLY FOR THE USA AND THE DEMOCRATIC VALUES THAT THEY REPRESENT AND PROTECT ALL AROUND THE WORLD. THE SANITARY AND TECHNICAL ADVICE FROM THE US VETERINARIANS ADDED TO OUR GASTRONOMICAL 'KNOW HOW' PERMIT US TO PRODUCE THE BEST EGGS FOR YOUR HAPPINESS. HAVE A NICE TASTE.

V. Slow-Cooked Hatred

The biggest event on the calendar that summer at the *KA* office was a brief official visit by the commander-in-chief himself—that loathsome draft-dodger Bill Clinton. I was relieved of my usual duties that week to help set up the chairs and ferry the media around.

The visit was little more than an Air Force One refuelling stop, but it was treated with the full measure of pomp and ceremony the military so excels at. Out on the Ramstein Air Base tarmac, a grandstand and podium were erected. There was a marching band, bunting, American flags in vivid abundance. Military institutions are more important than their current directors, and military chains of command are sacrosanct; Bill Clinton was, above all else, their commander-in-chief. You didn't have to like him, but you had to honour the office and respect the rank. And so the staff and families of the KMC turned out in full force to wave and cheer, even though I'd be surprised if even one in 10 had cast a vote for him.

Clinton, for his part, was his usual self during the couple of hours he spent out on the tarmac, easygoing and supernaturally charismatic. He shook hands, smiled broadly, said kind things about the soldiers in evocative language. In a brief ceremony, he was presented with a commemorative flight jacket—one of those stylish distressed-leather ones, like Tom Cruise wore in *Top Gun*. Then the marching band played, and Clinton went over and blew a few notes on the sax. Not long after, he was back on Air Force One.

I watched the AFN News coverage of the event that night. They did a sort of vox-pops segment—they did a lot of these on AFN News—asking one soldier after another what they thought of Clinton's visit. The replies were all awkward chain-of-command pauses, stiff lips, bland bureaucratic language. You had to show your respect for the chief, your patriotic loyalty to America. It's not about politics; it's about duty. You serve your president no matter what party he comes from. The subtext, though, was 100-proof contempt.

This is the kind of hatred that lurked in the corners of the KMC—slow-cooked stuff, meat falling off the bone, it'd been stewing so long.

VI. Northerners & Southerners, Part 2

At the *KA* office, my closest associate in terms of both age and general worldview was SrA Ray Gomez. He was Mexican American, and he was actually a year younger than me—20 to my 21—and over the course of the summer he expressed the most pointed curiosity about my untucked-shirt take on the whole USAF thing. Ray was from some little town in California's Central Valley—Santa Something—and I got the feeling he was starting to think he'd made a serious vocational error back when he was 18 and just desperate enough to escape Santa Something that he'd gone and joined the military. He would sometimes shoot these screw-yourself looks at the back of Captain Law's head, and he told me he had an eyebrow ring he wore to clubs on the weekends; Maj. Turner (no relation) would rib him about it at Training Days.

One of the first times he took me into his confidence was to wonder if I ever went out clubbing at the German discos in Kaiserslautern, the nearest big city, which I didn't. (I was much too punk rock to abide European techno.) Well, he explained, he and his buddies—all Latino—used to get nowhere with the local women when they introduced themselves as USAF soldiers. Lately, though, they'd started speaking to each other at the clubs only in Spanish, posing as tourists from Spain. Between that and the eyebrow ring, SrA Gomez informed me, things seemed to be going quite a bit better with the ladies.

Another time, when no one else was in the office, SrA Gomez sort of leaned over toward my desk with a conspiratorial nod. "What's Canada like?" he wondered. It was the only time anyone asked me that question all summer. My editor, Eddie, sometimes chided me when I inserted an un-American u into words like honour and colour, and the kindly woman who wrote human-interest features once thanked me personally, with something verging on a hitch in her throat, for what we had done to rescue the American hostages in Iran in 1981. (I told her don't mention it.) Only SrA Gomez, though, ever bothered to ask what Canada was like in its own right.

I answered with something mildly enthusiastic, noncommittal, a typically Canadian not-too-bad-eh? sort of answer.

He rolled closer in his office chair, turning something over briefly in his mind. "Yeah. But is it, like, more liberal than the US?"

"Oh, definitely," I answered, sort of nodding and rolling my eyes at the hair brushing my shoulders and my torn jeans and the rest.

"Yeah," he said, sighing, like I'd confirmed a long-standing rumour.

I didn't have it in me to explain that by USAF standards, Canada was pretty much Communist. I knew, as I'd known watching that kid peel his paper-on-paper fruit into bite-sized strips across the Grade 2 classroom's aisle many years before, that there were some gaps you just couldn't cross.

VII. Another Old Ball Game

A few days before the Israel–Jordan exhibition game, I'd attended a round-robin game between the KMC All-Stars and Poland. It was my first big-time Little League baseball game. The KMC All-Stars, American kids raised in baseball's heartland, are perennial European Little League Championship co-favourites, rivalled seriously only by Saudi Arabia, whose team is made up almost exclusively of the children of American expats. The KMC pitchers all had cannon-shot fastballs and curveballs that defied the laws of physics, the infielders could make a double play look like virtuoso ballet, and the batters could not only take you deep but also poke a high pitch down a baseline or into a gap. I've been to my share of professional ball games, and they didn't have much on these 14-year-olds.

Poland, by contrast, had only discovered baseball in the first giddy light let in by the collapse of the Iron Curtain four years earlier. The 1994 Polish squad showed up in hand-me-down uniforms and retread equipment the KMC team had donated to them after last year's tournament.

By the fourth inning, KMC had built up a lead well into double digits, and the Polish kids had long given up trying to get actual hits. Instead, they threw a celebration fit for a grand slam every time one of their players managed by some strange miracle to get his bat around in time to simply make contact with the ball as it whizzed by at 80 miles per hour. It was oddly heartwarming to hear such resilient good cheer in the face of what had to be one of the all-time hardest ass-kickings in baseball history.

As the KMC side came up to bat in the bottom of the fourth, there was nothing but third-stringers left in its batting order, and you could tell even those kids were trying as hard as they could not to tattoo yet another of the Polish kid's pitches into the stratosphere. After allowing another run or six across the plate, the Polish pitcher somehow managed to catch a KMC batter looking at a third pitch for the second out of the inning, earning a hearty championship-sized cheer from the Polish side. It seemed, though, that a close call was a close call, because a surprising number of the American parents started barking madly at the umpire from the stands, telling him to open his damn eyes and stay in the game and so forth.

Now, let me reiterate: the KMC All-Stars, most of whom had been playing baseball since they could hold a bat, had a lead so insurmountable they'd likely have gone on to win the game with their hands literally tied behind their backs. Whereas for the Polish kids, the basic rules of baseball had been known for less time than your average base brat's posting. And still, a substantial swath of the American parents felt real injustice at a close third-strike call.

The basic details of this scene weren't totally foreign to me—I'd seen my share of irate hockey moms and dads, howling for the ref's blood—but I was thrown by the tone of it all. If you were five goals up in the third period, your parents usually didn't dispute many questionable tripping calls. It was the same gap, perhaps, as the one between modest little CFBs and a great big American AB: same airplanes, same abundance of flags and insignia and uniforms, but one was full of guys like my dad who did their jobs, and the other was full of people saluting the commander-in-chief and arguing over barbeque and balls and strikes like the fate of the whole free world depended on it. Like they were auditioning for the role of action hero.

This was the closest I came that summer to some sort of grand metaphor for this outsized American presence on foreign soil: a ferocious ritual display of overwhelming force, carried out by reluctant children as their proud parents called from the sidelines for more blood. But that story certainly never ran in the *KA*—it would have been bad for morale.

ACKNOWLEDGEMENTS

Working as an editorial team had its pros and cons. Compiling and editing an anthology was more work than we could have fathomed, but being able to share that load was a blessing. The co-editing process challenged contributors, too. Each essay showed us something new about the home front. And all of the individual contributors worked hard to fit within our collective concept while sharing their personal stories and literary craft. We salute them!

The editors and contributors would like to acknowledge the support of the Province of Alberta through the Alberta Foundation for the Arts.

CONTRIBUTORS

Joan Dixon had written nine nonfiction books and many articles as a cultural historian before her teenaged son joined up and deployed to Afghanistan, prompting this more personal essay. It won an Alberta Literary Award in 2010 and was excerpted in *Chatelaine*. Joan is a full-time editor and researcher.

Ryan Flavelle joined the reserves in June 2001 while still in high school, becoming part of 746 Communication Squadron. After completing a BA in history at the University of Calgary, he began pre-training and deployed in 2008. Upon his return, Ryan was accepted into the Centre for Military and Strategic Studies, graduating in 2011. The same year, he published a memoir, *The Patrol: Seven Days in the Life of a Canadian Soldier in Afghanistan* (Harper Collins, 2011).

Michael Hornburg studied journalism and library science at the University of Missouri during the Vietnam War era. He pursued adventure in Europe and followed his future wife to her southern Alberta homeland in 1974. His love of Calgary's free-enterprise spirit kept him from making a career of writing, but since he lost his soldier son in 2007, he has spent more of his time writing, as well as painting and delivering speeches.

Barb Howard, daughter of a reservist, has published three novels as well as fiction and nonfiction in magazines. Her latest book is a short story collection, *Western Taxidermy* (NeWest Press, 2012). A version of Barb's essay "The Reservist" was published in *Alberta Views*.

Shaun Hunter is married to a former reservist. Her essays have appeared in *The Globe and Mail, Geist* and *FreeFall*. She has also written several biographies for young people. Shaun's current project, a book of creative non-fiction, takes her back down to her Calgary basement for more material.

Ellen Kelly is a writer, editor and creative-writing instructor living in Airdrie, Alberta. Her fiction and creative nonfiction have been published in magazines and anthologies. Ellen has twice been a finalist for the Jon Whyte Memorial Essay Prize. Her father was a member of the 137th Calgary Battalion, CEF (Canadian Expeditionary Force), during the First World War.

Jill Kruse is a seasoned journalist who writes and edits stories for *Ubiquitous: A Canadian Military Lifestyle Magazine* from her hometown of Fredericton, New Brunswick, where she is also busy raising three young daughters. Jill lost her husband, Greg (a 19-year veteran of the Canadian Forces), to the war in Afghanistan in December 2008.

Nancy McAllister, sister of a full-time soldier, previously worked as a section editor at the *Daily Express* newspaper in London. Her writings on the home front experience have been featured in the 2007 book *Outside the Wire* and in *Canadian Living* magazine. She is now a freelance writer formerly based in North Vancouver, now living in Denver, Colorado.

Melanie Murray grew up in the military town of Oromocto, New Brunswick, during the 1960s; her father was a soldier at CFB Gagetown. She has been living in Kelowna, BC, since 1987 while teaching English at Okanagan College and raising her two sons. This excerpt from her book *For Your Tomorrow: The Way of an Unlikely Soldier*, written about her nephew, is reprinted by permission of Random House Canada.

S.M. Steele is an award-winning poet. She tracked Task Force 3-09 (1PPCLI) as an official Canadian war artist from 2008 to 2010 and was recently commissioned by the Calgary Philharmonic Orchestra to write *Afghanistan: Requiem for a Generation*. She also received a major international award to write her Ph.D. thesis, "The Art of Witness: A Poet's Road to War," in Exeter, UK.

Kari Strutt made a trip to Vimy Ridge and stood again on the cold, wet ground where Canada was born. Children played on the grass during the service. Their parents tried to rein them in. "Let them play," Kari's husband murmured. "That's what the soldiers did it for." Exactly. (A one-time naval reserve musician, Kari is an award-winning short-story writer currently finishing her first novel.)

Captain (Retired) Kelly Thompson, daughter, granddaughter and great-granddaughter of soldiers, was the author of *Under Fire*, a blog for *Chatelaine*, detailing her experiences in the Canadian Forces and on the home front. Kelly is slowly adjusting to civilian life, although she continues to write about the military and the complexities of being a soldier. She is the owner of Keystone Text in Vancouver, BC.

Chris Turner, the son of a Canadian Air Force (CAF) fighter pilot, grew up on military bases from Cold Lake to Chatham to Baden-Soellingen, Germany. He is the author of three books (most recently *The Leap: How to Survive and Thrive in the Sustainable Economy*), and his magazine features have won seven National Magazine Awards. Chris lives in Calgary with his wife and two children.

Scott Waters is a former infantry soldier who has subsequently been selected as a two-time participant in the Canadian Forces Artists Program. He teaches and paints in Toronto, and his solo art exhibitions include Rodman Hall Art Centre, the Art Gallery of Southwestern Manitoba, YYZ Artists' Outlet and The Alternator Centre for Contemporary Art. His solo book, *In the Wake*, will be published by Conundrum Press in 2013.